Write Like Stephen King

A study guide focusing on the novel IT

MATTHEW MCGUINNESS

SPECIAL OFFER

A comprehensive set of exercises accompanies *Write Like Stephen King*. The 20-page workbook will walk you through the process of planning a novel in the style of Stephen King, and help you practise techniques specific to the horror genre.

To receive the writing exercises for FREE, all you have to do is sign up for my *Popular Fiction Masterclass* email newsletter. Turn to the back of the book now to find out how you can do that.

ABOUT THE SERIES

Popular Fiction Masterclass is a series of study guides designed to help writers learn from bestselling authors. Each book focuses on a single bestselling novel, explaining what makes it great and how to emulate it. To find out more, go to the following Web address.

http://popularfictionmasterclass.com/about/

ABOUT THE AUTHOR

Matthew McGuinness is a graduate of the prestigious Creative Writing MA at the University of East Anglia. He blogs on the subject of writerly craft and works as an editor and copywriter.

CONTENTS

Introduction   1

Summary of IT   3

1   A Toolkit for Terror   25

2   Thematic Layers   55

3   Character   79

4   Place and Time   101

5   Narrative Structure   125

6   Building Intensity   152

Conclusion   167

Appendix 1: Pattern and Theme   168

Appendix 2: Act-Structure Comparison   182

Special Offer   184

INTRODUCTION

It has always puzzled me that writers aren't encouraged to learn by consciously studying the masters.

Think about how painters and sculptors have traditionally learned their art. Until the early twentieth century, they'd study the work of great artists from the ancient world. The idea was to learn every gesture and nuance used by the ancient Greeks. And when you fully understood the craft and sentiment behind those great works of the past, you could begin creating your own original pieces, but always in a way that owed something to the spirit of the Greeks.

In my opinion, writers should learn their art in exactly the same way. That's why I started writing my series of *Popular Fiction Masterclass* books. Think of each one as a period of study in front of an Old Master painting – a preparation for creating original work, inspired by a great example.

And there can be few examples better than Stephen King. *IT* was his 22nd novel, and obviously the work of an accomplished author. Published in 1986, it instantly became the US bestseller and has spawned two movies as well as a TV adaptation. Its unforgettable 'scary clown' character, Pennywise, has insinuated itself into the imaginations of millions of people around the world. In the course of my commentary on *IT*, I will unpack some of the skills that allowed King to achieve this runaway popular success.

Like all of my *Popular Fiction Masterclass* study guides, this book begins with a full summary of the novel under consideration. After that, the chapters are arranged thematically. They provide in-depth analyses of six different aspects of Stephen King's writing, and end with a handy summary of key points.

Here are the areas that I'll be covering in this book.

- What are the essential techniques for creating terror?
- How do you make the reader feel they've had a profound experience?
- What do you need to consider when writing a group of protagonists?
- How naturalistic should horror novels be?
- How and why is the novel broken into different types of subdivisions?
- How do you ratchet up the intensity of the story?

But that's not all. If you sign up for my email list, you can also get access to a free set of exercises. These challenging and varied activities will help you put into practice the many lessons that you've learned from *IT*. They provide days, if not weeks of targeted writing practice and novel-planning activities. If you work through them all in a committed way, you will have gained valuable experience of a practical creative process, but, more importantly, you'll have a whole load of material that will feed directly into your novel. If that sounds good, go straight to the back of this book and find out how to get hold of the exercises.

SUMMARY OF IT

Part 1 – The Shadow Before

Chapter 1 – After the Flood (1957)

1. Derry is experiencing extreme rainfall. Young George Denbrough (Georgie) is playing in the street with a paper boat.
2. The boat was made by Georgie's brother William (Bill), who stutters. It is not a happy home, although Bill cares about his brother.
3. A clown in the drain kills Georgie.
4. The aftermath of the killing. The paper boat drifts out of town.

Chapter 2 – After the Festival (1984)

1. The murder of a gay man, Adrian Mellon, is reported to Derry police by his friend Don Hagarty.
2. Mellon was being bullied by local thugs, who are now being interviewed separately by police. One says he saw a clown at the scene.
3. Adrian had been enjoying festival amusements in Derry.
4. Another of the local thugs is asked by police to describe what happened between Mellon and his tormentors.
5. A direct description of the start of the aggression directed at Mellon.
6. The police cajole one of the thugs into saying more. They indicate that they don't like gays either.

7. A description of the Derry gay scene and the background to Mellon and Hagarty's association. Mellon had made a short trip to Derry but stayed after the two of them became involved.
8. Hagarty telling police that he couldn't make Mellon understand that Derry is a 'sewer'.
9. Hagarty trying to persuade Mellon to leave Derry.
10. The thugs continue telling police about the developing aggression towards the two gay men.
11. The attack on Mellon, described directly, including the appearance of the clown.
12. Hagarty confirms the presence of a clown appearance to the police.
13. A thug continues describing their attack to the police.
14. Continued direct description of the attack.
15. Partially through the police interview and partially by direct description, Hagarty's perception of the clown is given.
16. Hagarty confirms the presence of a clown in the face of police scepticism.
17. The police suppress the information about the clown in the interests of obtaining a prosecution.
18. A prosecution was obtained. The clown was not mentioned.

Chapter 3 – Six Phone Calls (1985)

1. Stanley Uris is Jewish friend of Bill Denbrough. He is ashamed of his religious identity. On receiving a phone call from someone called Mike, he suddenly and inexplicably commits suicide. The word 'It' is written on the wall in blood.
2. Richie Tozier is a successful DJ and another friend of Bill Denbrough. He uses manic humour to cover up his psychological suffering resulting from bullying. He receives a phone call from Mike Hanlon and agrees to return to Derry. He explains to an associate that a group that was formed years ago when something bad happened in Derry. They promised they would get back together if it happened again.
3. Ben Hanscom, a successful architect, has apparently also received the call from Mike. He explains to a barman that he used to be fat but lost a lot of weight.
4. Eddie, the head of a limousine company, is a hypochondriac and asthmatic. He also has an overbearing wife who resembles

his mother. Like the others, he has agreed to return to Derry, but has to tear himself out of his wife's clingy grasp.

5.   Beverly Rogan (née Marsh) is in an abusive relationship with a man called Tom. He beats her frequently and gets particularly violent when he catches her smoking. On receiving the call, Beverly turns the tables on Tom, thrashing him and leaving the house.

6.   Bill is now a horror writer – no longer stuttering. He is in Great Britain with his wife, who is acting in a movie. He has already received the call and decided to go to Derry.

Derry: The First Interlude

Excerpt from an unpublished history of Derry by the librarian. 'It' seems to return every 27 years, bringing a spate of dreadful killings on each occasion. Knowledge of its activities has been handed on by past librarians. But, in addition to the killings perpetrated by 'It', Derry is a violent place in general.

Part 2 – June of 1958

Chapter 4 – Ben Hanscom Takes a Fall

1.   1985. Ben travelling by plane – drunk. He remembers the end of school term in the summer of 1958.

2.   1958. A direct account of the end of school term in the summer of that year. Ben in his fat days. He secretly admires Beverly.

3.   Ben encounters Beverly but is overcome with shyness.

4.   Ben makes his way to the library, stopping to buy sweets. Food is like a friend to him.

5.   School bullies Henry, Victor and Belch decide to wait for him to emerge from the library so they can beat him up.

6.   Ben loves the library. Inside, he sees a poster concerning a spate of child murders. His mother has warned him not to come home late or wander around alone. His dreams have been invaded by images of the clown.

7.   Ben checks out his books and buys a postcard.

8.   Ben writes a haiku on the card but omits his name. It is for Beverly. He leaves the library to post it. The bullies are waiting for him.

9. An overview of Derry's geography, including the Barrens, the Kenduskeag Stream and the standpipe. Ben is thinking about Beverly, and then the clown, when he is attacked and chased by the bullies. He loses his library books as he is running through the Barrens. Henry also has an accident. Ben takes the opportunity to kick him and run away.

10. Hiding from the bullies, Ben hears a distant encounter between the bullies and some other kids. They have apparently been building a dam in the Kenduskeag and it has just been destroyed.

11. Still in hiding, Ben sleeps and dreams of something that happened to him in the past. After a gauche encounter with the female librarian, he started walking home but encountered the clown. He had to overcome a sense of paralysis before he could run away.

12. Having woken up, Ben encounters the other boys, Bill and Eddie, and their broken dam.

Chapter 5 – Bill Denbrough Beats the Devil – I

1. 1985. Bill, flying to the US on the supersonic aircraft Concorde, thinks about his speedy childhood bike.

2. 1958. A remembered episode when Bill rode his bike at top speed without a care for his safety.

3. Ben appears on the scene just after the dam built by Bill and Eddie has been destroyed by the bullies. All of them have been persecuted by Henry, Victor and Belch in the past. The dam builders ask Ben to stay and help. Eddie is having an asthma attack, so Bill offers to go and get his medication.

4. Bill unties his bike and prepares to ride off.

5. Riding at top speed makes Bill feel confident. It helps him leave behind the memory of his brother Georgie's death.

6. The asthma medication Bill picks up is actually only water.

7. Bill returns with the medication. They get to know one another and make a plan to build a new dam together.

8. An account of the coldness in Bill's house after the death of Georgie.

9. Bill opens a photo album in Georgie's room and encounters 'It'. A picture of Georgie moves and speaks, then the book bleeds.

Chapter 6 – One of the Missing: A Tale from the Summer of '58

1. 1958. A reminder that there has been a spate of child killings.
2. An overview of the killings, using news sources. Not all of them seem to be directly attributable to 'It'. Some are due to sadistic adults.
3. Eddie Corcoran is wandering in Derry because he was being abused by his stepfather. While wandering by the canal, he is killed by 'It' in the new form of the Creature from the Black Lagoon.
4. A kid called Mike Hanlon finds traces of Eddie's death. He is reminded of something that happened to him.
5. A description of Mike's hard but stable and loving rural childhood – the background to his experience. One day, he had gone to the cellarhold – an abandoned industrial site that he was warned off. There, he encountered 'It' in the form of a giant bird and only just escaped. It seems to have taken the form of a creature he saw in a Japanese movie. He couldn't bring himself to tell his dad.
6. Back at the scene of Eddie Corcoran's death. Mike disposes of the knife that he found.

Chapter 7 – The Dam in the Barrens

1. 1985. Eddie on the road, heading for Derry. He has become a rather obsessive character. He is struggling to remember things from his childhood. The image of a dark and threatening place comes to him, but he can't fill in the detail. However, the dam-building day stands out as a special time.
2. 1958. A direct account of Bill, Eddie and Ben preparing to build a dam. Stanley and Richie are coming on later. Stanley's Jewishness is discussed. Bill is the one with the dam-building know-how.
3. They start building. Ben explains that the pressure of the water will simply bed the structure in more firmly.
4. They eat lunch and discuss the attack on Ben. The issue of his weight comes up. They have to reinforce part of the dam. Richie and Stanley arrive.
5. The dammed river is beginning to flood the surrounding land. Richie's hyperactivity and funny voices are described in a retrospective account of his arrival at the Barrens. Stanley is

clearly much shyer. Everyone works together for a while, then they rest and smoke. Bill plucks up the courage to tell them about the manifestation of 'It' through Georgie's photo album. There is recognition in the faces of the others.

6. A summary of a story that Eddie tells the other boys. At an abandoned house on Neibolt Street, he encountered a syphilitic vagrant who propositioned him sexually then chased him as he rode away. The other boys help Eddie interpret the experience.

7. A direct account of how Eddie returns to the house on Neibolt Street. 'It' manifests as a terrifying creature that has adopted certain traits of the vagrant and utters the same sexual proposition.

8. The scene returns to the dam-building day. Eddie asserts the reality of the apparition. Ben responds by telling of his encounter with 'It'. Richie claims to be sceptical. Stanley clearly has had an experience but won't discuss it at first. When he does begin to tell the story, they are interrupted by the local cop, Mr Nell.

Chapter 8 – Georgie's Room and the House on Neibolt Street

1. 1985. Richie, approaching the end of his car journey to Derry, is surprised by a deer in the road. He recollects the dam-building day at the Barrens and its importance for bonding the group of friends.

2. 1958. Mr Nell has just turned up at the dam building. All of them are willing to take the blame. Mr Nell explains that the Kenduskeag is part of the sewage system of Derry, and the dam is causing the whole system to malfunction. He forces them to take it down.

3. Bill opens up to Richie about his feelings of guilt over Georgie's death.

4. Bill and Richie go to Georgie's room and look at the photo album again. 'It' is manifested through the photos once again.

5. They treat Bill's fingers, which were wounded by contact with a picture in the album. Now Richie believes something supernatural is going on.

6. Richie wants to go and see a horror movie with other kids. He negotiates with his sardonic father to do some jobs in exchange for money.

7. Richie calls several of the boys to invite them to the movie, but they can't come. He decides to call Ben, remembering that he seemed lonely.
8. Richie has a playful encounter with Beverly and invites her to the movie.
9. Richie, Ben and Bev meet up, but the boys are concerned that the bullies, Henry, Victory and Belch, will be at the movie too.
10. They spot Henry, Victory and Belch in the theatre. Two movies are showing: a Frankenstein movie and a werewolf movie. When they are finished, and the kids are leaving, the bullies confront them. Richie, Ben and Bev beat them off and head for the Barrens. Once there, they run into Bill.
11. Bill and Richie decide to go and check out the house on Neibolt Street where Eddie saw the threatening vagrant. Richie remains sceptical in spite of the photograph album experience.
12. They ride to the house on Bill's bike, Silver. They have his dad's Pistol with them.
13. The two boys arrive at the house and pluck up the courage to go under the porch, just like Eddie. For Bill, it's a mission to destroy the creature that killed Georgie. They break into the basement and encounter 'It' in the form of a werewolf. It chases them as they ride away.
14. Bill sees the creature as a clown. Suddenly, the street behind them is empty.

Chapter 9 – Cleaning Up
1. 1985. Flying towards Derry, Beverly recalls how, after leaving Tom, she ended up at her friend Kay's place. Kay is angry at the way Bev blames herself for the violence Tom inflicted on her. Bev dwells on memories of her dawning sexuality. In particular, she thinks about the night after the movie trip.
2. 1958. A direct account of how young Bev heard voices from the bathroom sink and saw blood gush out of the plughole on the evening after the movie trip. Her father couldn't see the blood. He hit her for making a fuss.
3. She wakes up the following day, notices the changes of puberty in her body and prepares herself to go and check the bathroom.
4. She does chores with her mother, then goes to the bathroom and finds that it is still apparently covered in blood.

5. Beverly, Eddie and Ben are involved in a game of pitching pennies. Beverly is insulted by another kid, but Eddie and Ben stick up for her.
6. Bev tells the boys about the blood in her bathroom. They decide to go and look.
7. The boys can see the blood.
8. They help to clean the blood away.
9. While washing the bloody cleaning rags at a laundrette, the boys tell their 'It' stories to Bev. Even Stanley begins describing a supernatural experience. It took place at the standpipe, which, it seems, is associated with the deaths of a number of children.
10. A direct account of Stanley's experience. While out birdwatching, he was drawn into the interior of the standpipe by a strange noise. Apparitions of drowned children show themselves and address him. He tries to ward them off by repeating a litany of bird names. Eventually, he manages to open the door and run away.
11. The kids decide to tell Bill. They also discuss the fact that the litany of bird names acted as a deterrent to the apparitions. Stanley is reluctant to look into the supernatural stories any more deeply, since he is afraid of losing his grip on reality.
12. Back at home, Beverly tries to measure the depth of the drain under her sink. The tape measure begins to run out by itself. It comes back up with blood on it.

Derry: The Second Interlude

The librarian writing again, in the 1980s. There have been more murders. He is prompted to call the group of kids who encountered 'It' in the 1950s. The text then transitions to a description of an event that seems to typify the evil in Derry – the mass murder of black people in a dance hall in 1937. The librarian reports his father's telling of the story. On his deathbed, the librarian's father revealed another detail – that, during the mass murder, he saw a manifestation of 'It' as a huge bird with balloons that enabled it to float. The librarian then describes how he woke from a slumber after writing the preceding text and found a balloon tied to his reading lamp.

Part 3 – Grownups

Chapter 10 – The Reunion

1. 1985. Bill is called by Mike, the librarian. He reports that their other childhood friends have come back to Derry too, apart from Stan. Bill takes a taxi to their meeting in a Chinese restaurant, reacquainting himself with the city on the way.
2. The meeting in the restaurant.
3. They acknowledge one another's professional successes, then share a toast to themselves – the Losers' Club – before eating a large meal. Ben tells how he lost weight after a bullying episode. Mike refers to Stan's suicide and begins updating the others on recent happenings.
4. Mike gives an account of recent murders, but also explains that there is a pattern of such events going back into the history of Derry.
5. Mike points out that they are all successful people as adults because they are troubled. However, they have forgotten much of what happened to them as children. Another pattern is mentioned: they are all childless. Richie explains how his fertility returned after a vasectomy – something that was incredibly unlikely. Bill, in his role as the leader, asks them to vote on whether they should try to kill 'It'. Everyone agrees that they should.
6. They open fortune cookies and find disgusting surprises inside, including an eyeball and a gigantic fly. They try to resist by ignoring the phenomenon. The waitress can't see any of the horrible things on the table.

Chapter 11 – Walking Tours

1. 1985. Ben takes a walk and reflects on how he, like other children, was able to incorporate terrifying supernatural events into his life. He has nagging mental images of a turtle and the word 'Chüd'. Revisiting the library, he has an encounter with a librarian who is clearly concerned about his presence in the children's library. He is then visited by the clown, who mocks him and accuses him of killing the child victims of 'It'.
2. Eddie is also wandering. He remembers Greta – a girl he adored – and visits a house near the Barrens where he played baseball with a group of kids that included the enormous bully, Belch Huggins. In the Barrens, he comes across a concrete

pipe and begins to recall details from the 1950s, including the fact that Belch was killed in that place. Eddie then sees terrifying apparitions of Belch Huggins, Greta and another kid called Patrick Hockstetter, all of whom are dead.

3. Beverly wanders to the house that was her childhood home. She does not even know whether her father still lives there. She finds a strange old woman living in the house. While drinking tea and talking with her, the old woman changes into a figure like the Hansel and Gretel witch, then the clown. Bev runs from the house.

4. Richie's wanderings take him to a bench by a statue of Paul Bunyan. He sits and reflects on his tendency to act the clown – a characteristic that has often got him into trouble. He recalls an occasion when, as a child in the 1950s, Henry, the bully, had pursued him to take revenge for a smart remark. Richie had stopped at the same bench to rest when 'It' suddenly attacked him in the form of the Paul Bunyan statue.

5. Bill does not see 'It' while he is wandering. He talks to a skateboarding child and finds his childhood bicycle in a second-hand shop.

6. Bill and Mike fix up the bike together. Bill drops a deck of cards that he is playing with and notices that there are two ace of spade cards, both face up in the dropped pile. Since finding the bike, Bill has been bothered by a phrase: 'He thrusts his fists against the posts and still insists he sees the ghosts.' Mike helps him remember that he often used to mumble the phrase as a child. It was an exercise that helped him overcome his stuttering.

Chapter 12 – Three Uninvited Guests

1. 1985. Henry the bully is in a mental hospital. He is hearing voices that tell him to go and kill the Losers' Club.

2. Henry is visited by an apparition of his bully friend from childhood, Victor, telling him, once again, to kill the Losers' Club. 'It' helps Henry to escape by attacking a guard, having adopted the form of a clown with a dog's face.

3. Bev's husband Tom visits her friend Kay. He uses violence and threats to make her tell him where Bev has gone. He also wants to know about her link to Bill Denbrough – a name he got from a book found in one of Bev's pockets. Once Tom has

left, Kay sets about trying to find Bev's hotel so she can warn her that Tom is coming.

4. She finds the hotel and leaves a message.

5. Tom flies to Maine. En route, he does some research into Bill and his wife. The fact that Audra looks like Bev makes him suspect that there may be something between Bill and his wife. At the airport, Tom buys a cheap truck. He is planning to find Bev and punish her. The punishment will include making her eat a carton of cigarettes.

6. Bill's actress wife, Audra, flies to Maine, concerned for her husband. She leaves the movie production she is working on in a mess.

7. She lands in the US and hires a car to drive to Derry. She is feeling terrified.

8. Tom and Audra are in different hotels but close to one another. Their cars are nose to nose.

9. Henry has escaped. He is heading for Derry.

Derry: The Third Interlude

Mike the librarian writing again. An account of a bloody 1930s episode. A criminal gang was gunned down by a large number of citizens (including a relative of Bill). The clown was seen shooting at the gang too, while floating above the street.

Part 4 – July of 1958
Chapter 13 – The Apocalyptic Rockfight

1. 1985. Bill remembers an occasion in childhood when the Losers' Club was at the Barrens together. He was feeling the burden of responsibility for deciding what to do about 'It'.

2. 1958. A direct account of the kids together in the Barrens, discussing what to do about 'It'.

3. A summary of events illustrating Henry the bully's hostility to the Losers' Club, but also to local black people. One target of his race hatred is the Hanlon family – Mike's people. Henry poisoned their dog and attacked Mike. His father advises him not to take a stand.

4. Bill's dad explains to him how the sewer system works – in particular the function of the concrete pipes that emerge in the

Barrens. Later Bill passes this information on to the other kids. He also tells them about some research he did. He believes 'It' is a type of spirit called a glamour, and that it can be expelled with an Indian ceremony called Chüd. All the while, they are being watched by 'It'.

5. Henry and his friends are in possession of some large firecrackers. They attack Mike, aiming to use the firecrackers to scare or harm him.

6. The Losers' Club are playing at the Barrens, imagining Tigers and Piranhas. They want to let off some firecrackers, but when they see someone working in the dump they decide to do it at a gravel-pit instead.

7. Mike is running from the bullies and finds himself cornered. Some of his pursuers are not as keen as their leader, Henry. Mike is bombarded with a firecracker and Henry taunts him with the revelation that he killed his dog. Mike runs again, heading for the Barrens. As the bullies close in, he turns and throws a lump of coal, which wounds Henry. He runs into the Barrens.

8. Playing with firecrackers at the gravel-pit, the Losers' club hear large explosions going off somewhere nearby. Bill fears that something is about to happen and begins collecting stones. The others, including Bev, follow his example.

9. Mike appears in the gravel-pit, followed by the bullies. An epic rock and firecracker-throwing battle ensues, and the bullies are forced to retreat. Mike introduces himself and is welcomed by the Losers' Club.

Chapter 14 – The Album

1. 1985. The group meets to talk and drink at the library, after hours. They are beginning to recall events related to their childhood confrontation with 'It'. Mike heads off to get a six pack of beer and finds the head of Stan Uris (as a child) in the refrigerator, together with balloons. The head mocks and insults him. Mike remembers when he first encountered 'It'.

2. 1958. The group of kids are together at the Barrens, planning the excavation of an underground club house. After a vote, Mike is accepted as a member of the group. They begin telling him how 'It' has been killing children.

3. After all the stories have been told, Mike tells them about his own encounters with 'It'. One was at a fourth of July parade. He also tells them that he saw a giant bird. It's a relief to share the memory.

4. Mike completes the story about the giant bird. They start digging the clubhouse. After leaving the Barrens, Ben, Richie and Bill discuss ways of getting rid of 'It'.

5. Mike comes to the Barrens carrying his father's photograph album. The group are having a laugh building the club house.

6. After a while, they notice Mike's album. It contains old pictures of Derry in which the clown can be seen. As with Georgie's pictures, the clown comes to life and tries to get at the children. Stan tries to deny what he has seen, but the others confirm that they all experienced the same thing and he eventually agrees. Bill believes 'It' is now afraid and vulnerable, but they must show courage

Chapter 15 – The Smoke-Hole

1. 1985. Back at the library gathering. Richie is feeling energised by the process of telling stories from the past. He wonders how it is that people lose their childish energy so suddenly. He felt something similar when he saved someone in an emergency situation. The group is remembering more and more detail from their childhood experiences. All of them agree that the things they saw were real – as real as the balloons and head in the refrigerator. Richie remembers that the cop, Mr Nell, interviewed them about another child murder soon after the photo album episode. He also begins to understand why he experiences a psychosomatic feeling of sore eyes. To explain, he begins telling a story.

2. 1958. The kids discuss some research they have been doing. American Indians used to have a ceremony that involved sitting in a smoky hole to induce visions. They decide to try it in order to help them decide how to deal with 'It'.

3. There is an attempt to exclude Bev from the ceremony, but in the end, they resort to drawing straws to see who will stay on guard. Strangely, the straws are all long. This is interpreted as a sign that they should all enter the smoke-hole.

4. The ceremony begins, but, one by one, the kids have to leave the hole. In the end, only Richie and Mike remain. Visions start to affect them.
5. The two boys find themselves in the same place, by the Kenduskeag, but millions of years ago. A strange object falls from the sky, and they understand that they are seeing 'It' arriving on Earth.
6. The other kids explain how they dragged Richie and Mike out of the hole semi-conscious. Richie and Mike give an account of the vision. The thing they saw falling was like the Ark of the Covenant, and it fell right where the city centre now is. That was how 'It' arrived, long ago. Since then it has been sleeping and, later, moving around in the sewers.

Chapter 16 – Eddie's Bad Break

1. 1985. Eddie finishes his account of the smoke-hole ceremony. Further details come back to the group, including the fact that all the bully kids died, apart from Henry. The balloons floating in the library suddenly show a message saying that asthma medicine causes cancer. This upsets Eddie. He starts to recall an episode connected with his aspirator.
2. 1958. A direct account of how Eddie was called into the office of Mr Keene, the drugstore owner, one day. Mr Keen explains that the medicine Eddie has been receiving is a placebo and that it is his mother who has the problem, making him anxious with her over-protectiveness. Eddie refuses to believe it at first but notices that the medicine packaging contains no safety warnings.
3. After leaving the drugstore, Eddie is attacked by Henry and Patrick Hockstetter. They even intimidate an adult who tries to intervene. Eddie's arm gets broken.
4. Eddie is driven to hospital. On the way, he sees the clown in the driving seat of the ambulance. His mother arrives and infuriates the medical staff with her interference.
5. Under the influence of painkillers, Eddie has vivid dreams that include his mother and the clown. He dreams of his own death.
6. Eddie's mother is visiting. She drives away the other members of the Losers' Club when they show up. She blames them for the broken arm, which makes Eddie furious with her. The

mother is powerfully affected by her son's new assertiveness. He also accuses her of lying to him about his asthma.

7. Eddie uses his aspirator as soon as his mother is gone, even though he accepts that it is a placebo. He reflects on the necessity of sticking together as a group of friends in order to overcome 'It'.

8. The Losers' Club returns to the hospital. They report that they are planning to make silver ammunition. Eddie reflects, once again, on the importance of friends. They sign his plaster cast and talk about a recent child murder. A thunderstorm is breaking but no rain comes.

Chapter 17 – Another One of the Missing: The Death of Patrick Hockstetter

1. 1985. Eddie finishes his story and prompts Bev to tell the group about the death of Patrick Hockstetter. She explains that she was alone at the Barrens when she spotted the group of bullies. She secretly watched them as they lit their farts.

2. 1958. A direct account of the story. She comes across Henry and his friends semi-naked in the quarry. Terrified and fascinated, she watches them.

3. A description of Henry's crude home life.

4. Bev watches from her hiding place as Victor and Belch leave Henry and Patrick alone. At Patrick's instigation, their game becomes sexual, until Henry suddenly turns hostile and leaves. Patrick turns his attention to an abandoned refrigerator.

5. An account of how Patrick murdered his baby brother and developed a taste for cruelty to animals, including locking animals in the abandoned refrigerator. The story has now reached the moment witnessed by Bev. Patrick opens the refrigerator and is attacked by strange flying leeches. 'It' drags him off to somewhere dark and damp and begins feeding on him.

6. Emerging from hiding, Bev is attacked by the flying leeches. Her attempt to kill one of them with her slingshot is apparently aided by a mysterious force. Near the refrigerator, she finds a lot of blood, an abandoned wallet and tracks that lead to one of the concrete pipes.

7. The Losers' Club are gathered at the refrigerator. Opening it, they find a message from 'It' written in blood. Bill rages against the creature that killed Georgie.

Chapter 18 – The Bullseye

1. 1985. Ben reveals a scar from his childhood encounter with 'It', which has recently returned. The group remembers preparing to make silver slugs.
2. 1958. A direct account of the research and resourceful activity that went into the preparations for making the silver slugs.
3. The actual making of the slugs.
4. The kids are waiting for the slugs to cool. Bev is worried that she will get into trouble. Ben fantasises about protecting her from her father.
5. The group plays Monopoly and Bev calls her mother. Bev experiences romantic feelings for Bill.
6. The slugs are ready. They plan where to hide them. Bill's mother is struck by a powerful atmosphere around the kids.
7. The kids arrive at the house on Neibolt Street where Richie and Bill previously encountered the werewolf. Eddie is with them again. They make ready to go inside.
8. With some difficulty, they enter the basement. As they move through the house, increasingly terrifying phenomena confirm the presence of 'It'. Bill tells Stan to use his litany of bird names to ward off evil, just as he did at the standpipe.
9. They come to a bathroom with an exploded toilet. This is where 'It' comes from. The creature comes rushing out of the filthy sewage pipe and appears as a werewolf. As they fight it, Ben is wounded. Bev shoots it with a slug, but it escapes.
10. In the aftermath of the fight, there is a moment of sexual tension between Bill and Bev that makes Ben feel jealous.
11. The sexual jealousy continues as they sit in the clubhouse discussing what they've just done. 'It' is clearly not dead and still represents a threat.
12. Two weeks in which nothing happened.

Derry: The Fourth Interlude

The librarian gives an account of a grisly mass murder in a bar in Derry in 1905. He originally recorded a very old local resident telling the story. Mike comes to the conclusion that monsters crave faith and imagination. But an act of faith can also make you a monster killer.

Part 5 – The Ritual of Chüd
Chapter 19 – In the Watches of the Night

1. 1985. Ben finishes telling his story. The group is daunted by the prospect of dealing with 'It' again. Bill's hands suddenly become covered in blood. In response they all hold hands, provoking a violent response – books flying off shelves and machinery taking on a life of its own. They head back to their accommodation. Bev and Bill seem about to spend the night together. Bev tells him a story about her father.
2. 1958. A direct account of Bev's story. She is beaten by her father for associating with boys and runs out onto the street, but people simply ignore her cries for help. Having evaded her father, she runs into Henry and the other bullies. Henry has a knife.
3. 1985. Mike stays at the library to clear up and write his journal. The rest of the group have gone to bed. Henry appears, with a knife. They are both badly wounded in the struggle that follows. He tries to phone for help, but the call is answered by the clown.
4. 1958. Back to Bev's story. Passers-by fail to help her. She kicks Henry in the balls and runs.
5. 1985. Bev and Bill make love. She remembers a sexual element to their battle with 'It' back in the 1950s.
6. 1958. Bev has run to the Barrens to get away from Henry and the others. She takes refuge in the clubhouse with Ben. When the bullies are gone, they talk about Ben's feelings for her. They also discuss the fact that Henry is apparently being controlled by 'It' – he has gone beyond all social norms.
7. 1985. Henry stumbling around Derry badly wounded and with a crazy internal monologue. He still wants to kill the other Losers. The moment when he lost Bev on the Barrens comes back to him.
8. 1958. A direct account of Henry and the other bullies at the Barrens. They wait for Bev and her friends to appear. An account is given of how Henry's knife had appeared in the mail, accompanied by balloons bearing the faces of the Losers'

Club. He killed his father with it. At that moment he began hearing voices urging him to kill the kids.

9. 1985. Henry gets a ride in a car driven by one of his childhood friends – now dead. Henry tries to explain away his role in the death. Details of the final confrontation in the tunnels below Derry emerge as he speaks to the corpse. They arrive at the hotel where the Losers are staying. 'It' has left a list of their room numbers in the glove compartment. He goes to Eddie's room first.

10. 1958. Richie, Stan and Eddie as kids, discussing religion. First Bill, then Mike, Bev and Ben catch up with them. Ben explains that Henry has gone crazy. They head for the Barrens. A storm is gathering.

11. 1985. A struggle between Henry and Eddie at the hotel. Henry is killed with a broken bottle.

12. 1958. At the Barrens, Bill understands that he led the group towards danger because nowhere at all is safe. Derry is 'It'. They are attacked by the bullies, throwing rocks. Retreating, they climb down into a concrete pipe. In the dark, trying to decide what to do, they discuss the Indian ceremony that reportedly overcomes glamour spirits – chüd – but it doesn't seem like a solution to their current situation. They head further into the tunnel.

Chapter 20 – The Circle Closes

1. 1985. Tom dreams that he is Henry in 1958 chasing the kids through the tunnels under Derry. A balloon is in his room when he wakes up, and a voice tells him what to do next.

2. Audra dreams she is Beverly in 1958, running through the same tunnels. Worried and beginning to hear the voice of 'It', she calls the hotel where Bill is staying. She fears he is having an affair when she finds he is not in his room. The clown appears on her TV set. She goes out to her car, planning to find Bill's hotel, but is intercepted by Tom.

3. Ben and Bill go to Eddie's room. The rest of the group are summoned together to deal with the fallout from Henry's death. Calling Mike, they discover that he has been attacked but survived.

4. The group decides that now is the time to attack 'It'.

5. They jump into Eddie's car and hear Georgie's voice on the radio, blaming Bill for his death.
6. They arrive at the Barrens with a feeling that a circle is closing. On reaching the concrete pipe, they discover Audra's handbag. They climb down into the tunnel.

Chapter 21 – Under the City

1. 1958. 'It' reflects on the unexpected threat represented by the children.
2. Wading through the drain, the kids come across the body of Patrick Hockstetter.
3. 1985. 'It' considers the current state of affairs. Audra is in the creature's possession and has realised that 'It' is female. She is somehow trapped within the creature's thoughts – in the deadlights. Tom died from shock on seeing the true form of 'It'. The Losers' Club, 'It' believes, now lack the childish imagination that previously posed a danger.
4. The group finds the rotted bodies of Victor and Belch, two of the bullies from their childhood.
5. Patrick Hockstetter's body is still where they left it in the 1950s. Nearby, they find Audra's wedding ring. Bill puts it on.
6. 1958. The kids are attacked by a giant eye. Eddie imagines his aspirator contains acid. He uses it as a weapon. Further on, they are attacked by the giant bird. Eventually, they come to a tiny door with a mysterious symbol drawn on it. The symbol evokes different traumas for each of them. They go through the door.
7. 1985. The group is approaching the same point in the tunnel system. They can't remember what they encountered there as children. Bill strikes a match.
8. All around Derry, strange, anomalous phenomena are occurring.
9. Bill sees Georgie coming towards him. The apparition accuses Bill of being responsible for his brother's death. It becomes monstrous in appearance. Bill finds he can ward off the creature by repeating the mantra that helped him overcome his stutter. It is finally dispelled, and Bill is able to express his sorrow over the death of Georgie.
10. A great flood is rising in Derry. Mike wakes up in hospital.

11. In the tunnels, the group feels that Mike is in peril. A power goes out from them.
12. Mike is attacked by a member of medical staff who is being controlled by 'It'. A surge of power from the other members of the Losers' Club helps him to resist until help comes.
13. They sense that Mike is safe. They turn again to the door. As when they were children, the symbol marked on it expresses a different fear for each of them. They encounter a monstrous spider that is not quite the creature's true form. Ben realises it is female. He receives a brief view of the real appearance of 'It'. What will come now is the ritual of chüd.

Chapter 22 – The Ritual of Chüd

1. 1958. A confrontation with the same spider creature. Bill forms a psychic connection with 'It' – the start of the ritual.
2. A psychic conflict between Bill and 'It', during which he encounters a turtle that created the universe. He triumphs in the chüd ritual by repeating his stuttering mantra. The spider creature is apparently dead, although the kids are not totally sure that they have completed the job.
3. 1985. Audra is unconscious – caught in the spider's web. A repeat of the psychic encounter between Bill and 'It' begins.
4. When it becomes clear that Bill has failed to make the connection required by the chüd ritual, Richie engages the creature. He and Bill are at the very edge of the deadlights, struggling to make their way back.
5. Now Eddie comes to the rescue. The spider and his mother seem to merge as he attacks with his aspirator. In the struggle, he loses an arm and dies.
6. Destructive events are occurring all over Derry.
7. 1958. Eddie, with his infallible sense of direction, led the group out of the tunnel system. There is still a nagging doubt about the finality of the victory over 'It' and the group already feels as though it is losing its closeness. Beverly believes that establishing a sexual bond between them will restore their unity.
8. 1985. This time they resolve to pursue 'It' until they have definitely killed it. Richie is distraught over Eddie's death, and Bill is afraid for Audra. He tries to rescue her from the web.
9. They crush the spider's young.

10. 'It' prepares itself to make a final stand.
11. Beverly dwells on a memory of birds that blots out the real events that followed the confrontation with 'It' in 1958.
12. 1958. An act of sexual union between Beverly and the others.

Chapter 23 – Out

1. 1985. An apocalyptic flood engulfs Derry.
2. Bill and Richie renew the attack on the spider. Bill tears its heart out, but Richie's fate is unclear. Bill carries him to safety.
3. The city begins to collapse.
4. Richie is not dead. He regains consciousness. Bill leads them back through the tiny door. They can no longer see a symbol marked on it.
5. The connection between the children's library and the adult library is blown apart, although, mysteriously, this is not because of the flood.
6. The group carries Audra out through the tunnels but has to leave Eddie's body behind. Water is gushing around them. They climb out of hole that has appeared in the city centre.
7. Derry tries to come to terms with the disaster that has occurred.
8. Bill, Richie, Ben and Bev put Audra in a passing ambulance. They remember how they emerged from the tunnels in 1958 and affirm their love for one another.
9. 1958. A direct account of the kids emerging from the tunnels. They have a new sense of positivity, but also loss - they know they have just left behind their old lives. They swear they will come back if 'It' is not dead.

Derry: The Last Interlude

1985. Mike's account of a conversation with Bill. They discuss the group's parting. Audra is still catatonic. Richie has gone back to Los Angeles, having expressed the view that the group will once again forget what they have experienced. Bev and Ben are planning to be with one another, but she shows signs of having forgotten Tom's ill-treatment of her. Bill says he is already forgetting details of their experiences in the tunnels. The bodies of Tom and Eddie will probably remain undiscovered below ground. Mike's memories are fading too. All the more important that the journal remains to remind people of what happened in Derry. The city still seems in the grip of a strange power – odd events are happening here and there that illustrate a turning away from the past. Mike's journal records the gradual ebbing away of the group's memories of one another.

Epilogue – Bill Denbrough Beats the Devil – II

1. Sometime after the 1985 confrontation with 'It', Bill is staying in Mike's place. He has a plan that he hopes will, at least, keep him connected with the events that led to Audra's catatonic state.
2. All is quiet in Derry.
3. He prepares his old bicycle for a ride.
4. He feels the time is right to put his plan into action. Through it, he will be taking leave of Derry and its influence.
5. With Audra on the back of the bike, he sets off at speed.
6. A reflection expressing the idea that you should not look back.
7. The danger of the ride brings Audra back to herself. Bill's stutter is also gone.
8. Bill dreams of his childhood.

1. A TOOLKIT FOR TERROR

'There was a clown in the stormdrain.'
– Stephen King, *IT*

It may seem like stating the obvious, but the defining characteristic of the horror genre is fear. It exists for no other reason than to scare readers witless, and any aspiring author of horror fiction must become a student of this art. As we'll see in the course of this book, a horror novel may also provide the reader with a lot of other very entertaining experiences, but they are ultimately secondary. Admittedly, there are other thriller genres that depend to some extent on making you afraid – crime especially, but also science fiction in some cases. It's also true that those genres sometimes share certain typical features of horror fiction – otherworldliness and freakish foes, for example. That's why fiction that crosses over between horror to SF or crime is extremely common. Even supernatural subject matter is no longer the exclusive property of the horror genre, since it can commonly be found in the young-adult and romance genres. But, unlike fiction in other genres, a horror novel truly stands or falls on whether it gets the reader looking over their shoulder at night or shivering in the sunshine. This chapter will examine some of the key techniques by which Stephen King achieves that effect in *IT*.

Content

To start with, I'm going to look at the basic elements of story –

character and action – and consider some fundamental ways in which they can be used to generate fear.

Anxiety

Stephen King's *IT* has affected the imaginations of readers and moviegoers to a truly extraordinary degree. Although the book isn't the origin of that familiar popular-cultural motif 'the scary clown', the notion that clowns are dark and threatening characters did take a much stronger hold on the popular consciousness after King's terrifying creation Pennywise reared his orange-tufted head in 1986. You would have to turn to the novel *Dracula* or the movie *Jaws* to find another horror creation that had been so successful in giving people's fears a new shape. And even then, there's clearly a reason to be scared of vampires or sharks. But a clown? What gives?

The clown isn't the only form taken by 'It', but it's certainly the guise that people remember. That's why publishers of the book and moviemakers responsible for the various adaptations have routinely used clown imagery in their publicity. It's clearly the most successful ingredient in Stephen King's recipe for fear, and the reason isn't difficult to see. People find clowns in general a mildly alarming mix of the anarchic and the pleasant. The unpredictable nature of these colourful, custard-pie-throwing creatures is without doubt unsettling. They're soppy but destructive, bold but vulnerable, physical but decorative. As a result, they leave children and adults alike with ambivalent feelings. When we're watching them, we feel the experience could go either way, tipping over into laughter or unpleasantness. It's that state of instability that makes them great raw material for horror. Naturally, no one runs in terror from a circus tent when they appear in the ring – we all understand that they're basically a safe and entertaining phenomenon. The point is that underneath the sweetness there's a potential for unpleasantness. The characterisation of Pennywise simply takes the alarming side and puts it on steroids, making it infinitely crazier and more terrifying than the reality.

This focus on semi-trusted aspects of life – drawing out and enhancing the features that are already slightly threatening – is a standard technique in the horror genre. Think of Hitchcock's movie *The Birds*, based on a story by Daphne du Maurier, with its terrifying sparrows, crows, seagulls and even chickens. Our feathered friends may not be an obvious source of danger in real life, but in large flocks they display a mysterious group intelligence. Their scaly feet, beady eyes and quick movements are also somewhat unpleasant. The movie takes those characteristics and turns up the volume on them until they become truly scary.

Consider, also, the 1976 supernatural thriller movie *The Omen*, which gradually reveals that Damian, a little boy with a mischievous glint in his eye, is in fact a satanic incarnation. It's something that one might say jokingly about a naughty child, that he's the devil incarnate. But in the movie, that slightly negative feeling towards a child is made concrete and larger than life.

Stephen King has deployed the same technique to great effect in a number of his novels. In *Cujo*, and *Pet Sematary*, for example, family pets are the source of fear. It's easy to see how some people develop negative feelings about dogs, for example, if they've been bothered by animals that bark and leap up, or if they've read a news story about a mauling. But this anxiety is usually something that exists under the surface of more positive feelings. The novels exploit that subterranean fear by dragging it out into the open and exaggerating it. In *The Shining*, it's a husband and father who turns into a monster. He displays an exaggerated version of the unpredictability and anger that can shake a child's trust in an otherwise loving parent.

Anxiety – the idea that our nagging fears will turn out to be completely justified – is a normal and natural reflex, just waiting to be triggered by a skilful writer of horror stories. Originally a survival instinct, anxiety has stayed with us to the present day, manifesting itself in perfectly ordinary circumstances. In fact, most members of the human race experience the same kind of anxieties at the same stage of personal development. As toddlers, we're worried about abandonment by our parents. Child psychologists believe it stems from early experiences of separation from our parents, which instils a fear that protection and care might be withdrawn at any moment. Significantly, toddlers are not usually anxious about the many obvious sources of danger in their lives – things such as crossing the road or the consequences of pushing random items up their noses. If anything, those kinds of experiences have a frisson of excitement. Instead, their nightmares focus on the suspected precariousness of their situation. Older children or teenagers tend to be afraid of things like social rejection at school – the suspicion that their friends will suddenly turn nasty on them if they do something uncool. Once again, it's not the obvious dangers like climbing trees or experimenting with cigarettes that cause them anxiety. Those things are considered rather exciting. Then, as we enter adult life and start a family, fears for our children predominate – specifically, fears about the people and things we trust to entertain and protect them. The anxiety that something bad will happen as soon as they're out of sight or left in the charge of carers is universal. And you can add to that the many fears artificially created and fuelled by the media – thoughts that we may be inadvertently harming our children by making the wrong nutritional or educational choices on their behalf.

One factor behind the terrifying effectiveness of Pennywise is that the idea of a child-murdering clown taps into this reservoir of anxiety about child rearing. Stephen King supplies a scattering of details that encourage us to see the character in those terms. When Georgie encounters Pennywise in the drain, he's reminded of two children's television characters from the 1950s: Bozo and Clarabell. It's also noted that Pennywise is wearing 'white gloves, like the kind Mickey Mouse and Donald Duck always wore.' So, in the run up to the boy's grisly murder, we are being reminded of televisual experiences that formed the background to most children's lives in the Western World for more than half a century. This is not accidental. In an even clearer statement of purpose, Stephen King writes that 'If George had been inhabiting a later year, he would have surely thought of Ronald McDonald.' In its details, the characterisation of Pennywise draws on those aspects of childhood that parents typically feel most ambivalent about: TV, movies, fast food – trashy popular culture in general.

The horror genre is full of movies and novels exploiting the same fears. For example, in the 1982 movie *Poltergeist*, the television becomes a channel for communication between a little girl and malevolent spirits. The memorable image of the child staring into a hissing TV screen crystallises that anxiety, just like the cartoonish characterisation of Pennywise. The anxiety is then amped up for horrific effect when the child disappears into the dark world behind the screen. It's an equivalent of Georgie's murder, which turns up the volume on the same set of parental fears. Interestingly, when the movie was remade in 2015, the publicity images didn't revolve around the image of a TV, but rather a 'scary clown' toy that plays a minor role in the paranormal events of the story. It's a testament to the power of that particular image to tap into a common set of fears.

Nightmare

We've just seen how most human beings have an 'anxiety button' in their heads, which can be pressed at will by a skilful storyteller. But the unconscious mind has an endless supply of these ready-made fear responses. You only have to dip into your dream life to gain access to them. Stephen King is clearly no stranger to the murky depths of the mind, because his novels are littered with imagery and scenarios that are all too familiar from nightmare. Let's consider one such motif.

In Chapter 6, section 3, we meet Eddie Corcoran – a troubled kid hanging out in a park by the canal. He's destined to suffer a grisly death at the hands of 'It'. While he's sitting at the water's edge reflecting on his life, a hand reaches out and grabs his foot. As you might expect, he makes a run for it. But as he tries to escape, the creature chasing him morphs into a terrifying sea creature, and he just can't seem to get away.

> Something was following him. Eddie could hear it bludgeoning its way through the willow grove. If he turned he would see it. It was gaining. He could hear its feet, a kind of shuffling, squelching stride, but he would not look back, no, he would look ahead at the light, the light was all right, he would just continue his flight to the light, and he was almost there, almost –
>
> …
>
> Eddie put on a burst of speed.
>
> …
>
> The stink. The overwhelming stink of it. Gaining. All around him. It was a park bench he tripped over.
>
> …
>
> He looked behind him and saw the creature bearing down

We're told that the pursuing creature makes a shuffling sound, suggesting that it's moving slowly. Eddie also seems unable to find any speed – he's said to be 'almost there', but never quite reaches safety. And the pace of the writing emphasises the slowness of the movement by providing all sorts of extra information during the chase. We're told, for example, that he thinks about drinking a cup of coffee and listening to a Buddy Holly song. This is the literary equivalent of slow motion. But then we're then told that Eddie is putting on a burst of speed. Surely he must escape. Not so. He runs straight into a bench and the creature gains on him remorseless. It's as though there's nothing he can do to escape his fate.

We've all had nightmares along those lines. It's one of the most common ways in which our mind acts out feelings of helplessness – a scenario of trying to run away from something while being held back. The harder you try to escape in such dreams, the more you find yourself bogged down, tangled up or impeded. Chapter 9 section 10 uses a similar effect. We find Stan at the standpipe. In this haunted setting, doors lock themselves, preventing escape, and the number of steps in the stairway increases as he tries to run down them. It's the same kind of nightmare.

In section 5 of Chapter 3, we see another technique that's closely related. After receiving a call from Mike Hanlon asking her to return to Derry, Bev has hit back at her husband – literally – leaving him bruised and bloody on the floor. But he's not quite down and out yet. He pulls himself together and begins shouting wildly while Bev is packing a suitcase downstairs. He could come down the stairs at any moment. The important aspect of this episode – the thing that injects real fear into it – is the fact that Bev has a task to complete before she can get away from the threat. She has to pack the bag and get some clothes on. Stephen King deliberately describes each trivial step, building our anxiety.

> At the foot of the stairs she grasped the hem of her white lace nightgown cross-handed and pulled it over her head. It was bloody, and she would not wear it one second longer, no matter what. She tossed it aside and it billowed onto the rubber-plant by the doorway to the living room like a lacy parachute. She bent, naked, to the suitcase. Her nipples were cold, hard as bullets.
> …
> She gasped, jerked, then bent back to the suitcase. If he was strong enough to scream that loud, her time was a good deal shorter than she had thought. She opened the case and pawed out panties, a blouse, an old pair of Levi's. She jerked these on standing by the door, her eyes never leaving the stairs.
> …
> She jabbed the buttons of the blouse through the holes as fast as she could. The top two buttons were gone (it was ironic how little of her own sewing ever got done) and she supposed she looked quite a bit

like a part-time hooker looking for one last quickie before calling it a night – but it would have to do.

King also punctuates the episode with reminders of the looming threat.

'BEVERLY YOU GET YOUR ASS UPSTAIRS!'

Anxiety-building chase episodes like these are a very common feature of horror fiction, as you're no doubt aware. But it's worth reflecting on the reason why these scenes give rise to such a powerful fear response in the reader. It all goes back to that common psychological phenomenon – the nightmare of running away but finding yourself held up. A writer of horror fiction needs to be a student of the unconscious.

Metaphysics

It seems to me that an important feature of successful horror stories – especially those that revolve around supernatural events, like *IT* – is the fact that they provide readers or viewers with a convincing and consistent explanation of the evil affecting the fictional world. That might involve scientific background information in the case of a disease-epidemic story, for example. In the case of a zombie story, it might include information about how zombies come into existence, what they're capable of and how they can be killed. In supernatural horror, there probably won't be much scientific or strictly factual information connected with the subject, but the need to be convincing and consistent is just the same. The term I like to use for explanations of supernatural phenomena is 'metaphysics'. The metaphysics of each horror story will be somewhat different. For example, one novel or movie in the genre might revolve around an assumption that ghosts are dead people trying to get justice for something that happened to them while they were alive. Another story might be based on the idea that ghosts are dead people roused from their sleep by the actions of the living – maybe when their burial place is disturbed.

Why is it so important to readers that they acquire a detailed understanding of the evil that they're reading about? Doesn't knowledge drive out fear? In fact, exactly the opposite appears to be true in the horror genre. For one thing, if the world you're reading about has no rules, it's difficult for the author to make you anticipate a specific threat. In fiction, chaotic danger loses focus and all too easily becomes laughable.

But there's another reason for the specificity with which the supernatural is described in *IT*. It's hinted at in Chapter 9, section 11, when we witness Stan encountering some ghostly children at the standpipe. The narrator explains the effect on Stan's state of mind.

> … those dead boys who had lurched and shambled their way down the spiral staircase had done something worse than frighten him: they had offended him.
>
> …
>
> It's offense you maybe can't live with, because it opens up a crack inside your thinking, and if you look down into it you see there are live things down there …

This breaking of the rational faculties is what Stephen King seems to be gunning for in relation to his readers. By insisting on the intellectual coherence of supernatural experiences, he wants to open up a crack in our thinking – a split between lived experience and plausible imagination. When that happens, fear comes flooding in.

So, what are the metaphysical resources available to authors when trying to create a wholly fictional but wholly concrete and convincing depiction of evil?

In spite of the widespread assumption that religion is dead in the West, its basic metaphysical assumptions are very much present in the horror genre. Our imaginations still respond powerfully to ideas such as demonic possession, as one can tell from the runaway success of movies like *The Exorcist*.

But that's not the whole story. Official religious thinking has always had areas of vagueness in its metaphysical account of the universe, and a speculative folk-metaphysics has cheerfully flowed into these gaps over the centuries, satisfying people's curiosity and emotional needs. The result has been a colourful variety of extremely fluid beliefs about the nature of supernatural phenomena. Many have been with us for centuries, if not millennia. For example, in the 14th-century Byland Abbey manuscript fragments, a number of ghost stories have come down to us. There is a ghost who wants to reveal the location of an item that he stole in life. There is also a ghost who maliciously harms the living. There is even a helpful ghost who wants to carry a load for a traveller. In Shakespeare's *Hamlet*, various understandings of the ghost of Hamlet's father are entertained. In the first sighting, Horatio speculates that it has some significance for the state as a whole, since it is an unrecognised man in armour. Hamlet later sees the ghost and recognises it. He is initially persuaded that it's his father in search of revenge. Later, however, it occurs to him that it might be a demon posing as his father.

There is rarely anything new in the world of metaphysical speculation. All of the historical ideas about ghosts that I described above have direct equivalents in modern movies and horror novels. The same goes for ideas about other supernatural phenomena with equally deep roots: vampires, werewolves, golems, demons and all the rest of it. The various longstanding beliefs about these phenomena may get a new twist from time to time in modern expressions, but in essence they remain the same. The vampires in Stephen King's *Salem's Lot*, for example, are slightly novel in that their human personalities get reflected in their subsequent vampire characteristics, but they're still averse to crosses and fire, as in historical descriptions.

Just occasionally, we see an aspect of horror metaphysics that's unprecedented. This usually signals a major shift in our circumstances as a culture. It would be surprising if something as huge as the birth of broadcast digital media hadn't thrown up something new, and indeed it did. One particularly memorable example is Koji Suzuki's novel *Ring*, and the movie adaptations, in which a cop comes across a video tape that kills everyone who watches it.

While you're reading *IT*, the metaphysics of the novel can seem elusive and even inconsistent. It brings together a vast range of supernatural beliefs. Aspects of the Christian tradition are hinted at, for example in the First Interlude, where Mike recounts how a man told him about the voices his wife heard from a plughole.

> ... all these voices answered back, she said – grunts and babbles and howls and yips, screams and laughin, don't you know. And she said they were sayin what the possessed man said to Jesus: "Our name is Legion," they said.

There are also borrowings of familiar folk beliefs. Some of these are quite prominent, like the werewolf manifestation of 'It'. Others are quite subtle, like the observation that 'It' has no shadow, recalling one of the traditional characteristics of vampires.

What appears to be an inconsistent jumble of ideas in fact turns out to have a coherent metaphysical explanation, which is clearly stated for the first time in Chapter 10. The members of the Losers Club, gathered at their reunion in a Chinese restaurant, are seeing grotesque things emerging from fortune cookies. Bill puts his finger on what it is that's happening.

> 'I've been thinking about writing a bug story,' he said. 'That Langlahan story had woven itself into my thinking. And so I saw a fly.

In other words, 'It' is drawing on the heroes' imaginations to create all those apparently unrelated manifestations. This particular piece of horror metaphysics is not unfamiliar from other novels and movies. Orwell's *1984* contains a version of the same idea: a torturer who has access to your innermost fears and won't hesitate to inflict them on you. The 1984 movie *Ghostbusters* plays the same thing for comic effect as the destructor adopts the form of Mr Stay Puft, a marshmallow man that one of the ghostbusters had just been thinking about. But Stephen King gives it a twist of his own. In a surprising chapter that adopts the viewpoint of 'It', we hear that the creature craves imagination as a delicious food, and yet fears it as a potential threat.

> It had discovered a depth of imagination here that was almost new, almost of concern. This quality of imagination made the food very rich. Its teeth rent flesh gone stiff with exotic terrors and voluptuous fears: they dreamed of nightbeasts and moving muds; against their will they contemplated endless gulphs.
> …
> Perhaps because they were children their imaginations had a certain raw power It had briefly underestimated.

The most important thing about this metaphysical idea underlying the novel is that the author reveals it gradually, in small increments. After the encounter with Pennywise in Chapter 1, it's quite a while before we discover that 'It' can take different forms and show itself in different ways. The swamp creature and the bird appear in Chapter 6, then, in Chapter 8, the photo album comes to life and the werewolf is seen for the first time. In Chapter 9, the apparitions of drowned children appear at the standpipe. Finally, in Chapter 10, at almost exactly the midpoint of the novel, Bill suggests for the first time that 'It' is plundering their imaginations. Some readers may have begun to suspect as much already, but it's only stated openly around half way through the story.

The metaphysics continue to deepen in the same gradual way right to the end of the novel. We have to wait until Chapter 21, section 1, to learn <u>why</u> 'It' is drawn to the imaginations of children – the fact that it is driven by a greedy craving for a delicious food.

And that's just one aspect of a dramatic enlargement of the metaphysical background to the story in its second half. In Chapter 15, Richie and Mike go on a visionary journey back to the arrival of 'It' on Earth. They learn that, having come from outside our universe, 'It' chose to create an image of its own viciousness in Derry.

In another development, chapters 15, 16 and 21 mention the existence of a mysterious positive force called 'the Turtle'. Up to that point, the image of a turtle had only flitted through the text now and again – hinted at in a very indirect fashion. This positive force is encountered directly in Chapter 22, section 2, during the kids' showdown with 'It'. Then, during the adults' struggle with the same enemy, in section 4 of Chapter 22, the Turtle is declared to be dead, deepening the metaphysical picture still further.

But the ultimate expansion of the metaphysical background is Bill's trip into 'the deadlights'. It's a place or state that's so removed from normal life and so transcendently terrifying that Stephen King chooses to describe it in only the vaguest terms.

Incredibly distant; incredibly far out in the black.

Most of the metaphysical insights that Stephen King drip feeds to us over the course of the novel are not so grandiose. He makes sure that we receive a steady flow of fascinating but less earth-shattering information. This often adds some new dimension to the characteristics and capabilities of 'It', such as the fact that only children can see and hear the creature's manifestations, or the fact that it has no shadow.

Sometimes, the drips of information relate to things that can be used as weapons against 'It'. For example, Stan discovers that he can deter the supernatural by repeating an incantation of bird names, and Eddie discovers that his inhaler, filled with harmless water as it is, will have the effect of acid if he simply convinces himself that it will.

The interludes are a particularly rich source of metaphysical details. Mike's research reveals, amongst other things, that child murders and random acts of violence have been going on in Derry for centuries, and that they occur in cycles of about 27 years.

These minor metaphysical insights may initially strike the reader as insignificant, but all of them turn out to be hints at the bigger metaphysical picture – the idea that 'It' feeds off (but also fears) the imaginations of children. The regular appearance of such details is fascinating to readers. It contributes to the concrete and convincing depiction of the supernatural, which, as we have seen, opens up cracks in a person's thinking, allowing fear in.

Structure

Now we turn our attention to the various ways in which Stephen King structures the story of *IT*. Together, these storytelling techniques form the skeleton that supports the novel's content, but most readers will only be dimly aware of them on a conscious level. Nevertheless, they also have a role to play in generating fear.

Build-up

It's a feature of many popular fiction genres, especially action-based ones, that the story increases in intensity as it progresses. There's a whole chapter devoted to this set of related techniques below, but I'd like, at this stage, to discuss the supernatural aspects of story intensification as I believe it's one of the most important contributors to fear levels in *IT*. Specifically, it seems to me that there's a steady increase in the frequency with which the supernatural appears in the novel's main narrative. Let's look at how that effect develops.

To begin with, there's a burst of 'It' appearances in the main narrative (i.e. not in the interludes but in the standard story chapters). Chapter 1 is the first time we see the creature up close in a directly narrated incident – the account of Georgie's murder.

Then, in Chapter 2, various characters describe Adrian Mellon's murder and the clown's role in it. It may not be a direct narration of an encounter with 'It', but the details are quite extensive and vividly described.

That is the end of the initial burst of appearances. We then don't see a directly described encounter with 'It' for quite some time. The creature doesn't appear at all in Chapter 3, although its presence is felt through Stan's suicide. In Chapter 4, it is only briefly mentioned as a feature of Ben's dream. Once again, it's not seen at all in Chapter 5, although Bill experiences the supernatural in the form of a moving, talking photograph of Georgie. Finally, in Chapter 6, we receive a direct account of an 'It' appearance once again, when Eddie Corcoran is killed by a sea monster. That's an interval of four chapters.

Now skip to the end of *IT*. The picture is quite different. In Chapter 21 alone, there are six separate appearances of 'It', three of which are directly narrated encounters. First, we hear a reflection by the creature itself as it considers the threat posed by the children in 1958. Later, we hear a similar reflection on the threat posed by the adult Losers in 1985. As the kids make their way through the tunnels in 1958, they're attacked by an enormous eye. Then, in 1985, 'It' takes the form of Georgie. While all this is going on in the tunnels, Mike is attacked in hospital by a staff member under the control of 'It' – not a direct encounter with the creature but a potent display of its influence. Finally, 'It' manifests itself to the adult Losers as a spider. All this takes place in just one chapter! The tempo of appearances has become a rapid staccato.

But what were the stages involved in that transition from slow to rapid tempo? Here's a timeline of all the novel's manifestations of the supernatural.

PART 1
Chapter 1:
- Georgie

Chapter 2:
- Adrian Mellon's murder

Chapter 3:
- Stan writes 'IT' on the wall as he kills himself

PART 2

Chapter 4:
- Ben has been dreaming of 'It'

Chapter 5:
- Photograph of Georgie talks

Chapter 6:
- Sea monster kills child

Chapter 7:
- Neibolt Street leper

Chapter 8:
- 'It' is manifested in a photograph again
- Neibolt Street werewolf

Chapter 9:
- Blood in Bev's bathroom
- Stan at the standpipe

PART 3

Chapter 10:
- Nasty things in fortune cookies

Chapter 11:
- 'It' appears to Ben at the library
- Bev in the Hansel and Gretel house
- Paul Bunyan attacks Richie

Chapter 12:
- Henry visited by 'It' in the mental hospital

PART 4

Chapter 13:
- Nothing

Chapter 14:
- The Losers are haunted by a severed head and sinister balloons in the library
- Mike seeing 'It' at a parade
- Mike encountering a big bird
- The Losers see 'It' in old pictures of Derry

Chapter 15:
- The arrival of 'It' on Earth

Chapter 16:
- The Losers see a message on the balloons in the library
- A clown ambulance driver appears to Eddie
- Eddie dreams of his mother and 'It'

Chapter 17:
- The fridge in the Barrens

Chapter 18:
- The attack on Neibolt Street

PART 5

Chapter 19:
- Henry attacks Mike in the library
- How Henry received his knife in the mail along with balloons
- Henry is driven by 'It' in the form of a dead friend
- Henry attacks Eddie at the hotel

Chapter 20
- Tom has dreams sent by 'It', sees a sinister balloon and hears the voice of 'It'
- Audra is haunted by 'It' via her dreams and the TV set
- Audra is attacked by Tom at the command of 'It'
- Bill hears Georgie's voice on a car radio

Chapter 21:
- 'It' reflects on the Losers in 1958
- 'It' reflects on the Losers in 1985
- An enormous eye attacks the Losers
- 'It' appears in the form of Georgie
- Mike attacked in hospital
- The spider in 1985

Chapter 22:
- The spider in 1958
- The spider in 1985
- Another reflection by 'It' in 1985

Chapter 23:
- The spider in 1985

Four important points suggest themselves.

1. The overall number of encounters with 'It' per chapter increases over the course of the novel.
2. Although the early chapters contain a few direct encounters with 'It', they contain more encounters that are fleeting, second-hand or mediated through phenomena such as a speaking photograph. In later chapters, by contrast, direct encounters are more predominant.
3. The direct encounters become more extended in nature. This is particularly pronounced in chapters 17, 18 and 21-23. The climactic encounters (with the spider) in chapters 21-23 are ultra-extended in nature, spanning many sections.
4. The climactic confrontations are also preceded by a group of shorter encounters with the supernatural in Chapter 21.

Suspense

Suspense is naturally one of the keys to success in a fear-based genre like horror. Alfred Hitchcock once defined suspense in the following terms. He said you must first show the audience a ticking bomb under the table, then you must show them the people sitting around the table chatting.

This is a great way of describing the first form of suspense in *IT* that I want to discuss. You could call it 'long-term' suspense because it's felt over long stretches of the story. Creating it requires two things to happen. Firstly, the reader must see that the main characters are dangerously exposed to some negative situation. Secondly, the reader must see that the only way of resolving that negative situation is for the main characters to achieve a certain goal. In the early chapters of *IT*, a lot of effort goes into setting up a feeling of terrible malaise hanging over the Losers. This is the equivalent of Hitchcock's bomb – the urgency factor. It's not just about the clown who we see prowling around Derry – that peril could easily be avoided if the protagonists just stayed away from their home town. Rather, the sense of malaise is about the profound and lasting effects of the Losers' childhood encounter with 'It'. Chapter 3 really goes to town on showing us how far-reaching and serious the consequences of that early trauma have been. Stan's suicide, during which he scrawls the word 'IT' on the wall in blood, has a particularly electrifying effect on the reader. But Bev's experience also contributes strongly to our sense of emotional urgency. Even as the author is planting this emotional bomb, he is also suggesting to us exactly how the Losers can overcome their malaise. They need to confront and defeat 'It'. Mike's telephone calls to his friends asking them to return to Derry are the key means of setting up that goal, and the Losers immediately become focused on the task. Bev, in particular, is transformed into an unstoppable force.

> 'Don't you ever try to grab something away from me,' he said hoarsely. 'You hear me? You ever do that again and you'll spend a month pissing raspberry juice.'
> 'Tom, stop it,' she said, and her very tone infuriated him – she sounded like a playground monitor talking down to a tantrumy six-year-old. 'I have to go. This is no joke. People are dead, and I made a promise a long time ago –'

The Losers' keen focus on a goal differs from the idleness of Hitchcock's idle diners, but it does nothing to detract from the suspense generated by their situation. That's because, as yet, the task of defeating 'It' seems impossibly tough. The more difficult the goal and the more powerful the urgency factor the greater the suspense will be. Stephen King takes deliberate steps to signal the riskiness of the goal as soon as it's revealed. In Chapter 3, section 6, for example, we see an interaction between Bill and his wife, Audra. He has just been asked by Mike Hanlon to return to Derry, but when Audra asks to go with him, his fearful reaction is striking.

> 'Take me with you, then.'
> The expression of horror that dawned on his face then – not horror of her but for her – was so naked that she stepped back, really afraid for the first time.

Now we really fear for these characters who we are already starting to like and empathise with. So much so that we just have to follow them to the end of their struggles. That's really the function of this kind of long-term suspense: to keep us on tenterhooks of dread, desperate to know that our fictional friends will be OK in the end.

In addition to creating a long-term feeling of suspense, Stephen King creates peaks of suspense around individual appearances of 'It'. These tense scenes conform to a pattern that's well worth analysing and emulating.

The scene in which Georgie encounters Pennywise is a good example. The key stages of the scene are as follows.

1. Normal human events and information about setting.
2. Ambiguous details that could be supernatural but could equally be down to an overactive imagination on the part of the viewpoint character.
3. 'It' reveals itself openly and clearly.

Let's look at the stages in more detail to understand how the suspense is created.

In the lead-up to Georgie's death, we see him playing with a paper boat in stormy weather and hear how his brother made the boat for him. It's very natural and charming. However, the atmosphere changes when we're told that Georgie is reluctant to go down the cellar stairs to get an item for the boat. He knows his fear of monsters in the dark is just his imagination, but the narration refers to the 'imaginary' monster as 'It', which has our antennae twitching nervously. From this point on, there's a deliberate ambiguity to the text. Details help to suggest the presence of something otherworldly without actually revealing it. For example, the weather is creepily personified in phrases such as 'rain swept restlessly against his bedroom window', and we're given a few gory details about bodies decomposing in the sewers after previous storms, all of which inclines us to read with a horror mindset. Our suspicions of a supernatural presence are extended for many pages in this way. The sense of anticipation is wound tighter and tighter until, finally, the author brings us face to face with a clown in a drain. Now the writing takes on a crystalline clarity, driving away all ambiguity.

> The face of the clown in the stormdrain was white, there were funny tufts of red hair on either side of his bald head, and there was a big clown-smile painted over his mouth.
>
> …
>
> The clown held a bunch of balloons, all colors, like gorgeous ripe fruit in one hand.
>
> In the other he held George's newspaper boat.

The development of this passage is the essence of suspense –

hinting at the presence of something horrifying but withholding its appearance for as long as possible. Or, to put it another way, the author is showing us the bomb but withholding full character awareness of it.

Another instance of the same scene structure can be found in section 3 of Chapter 6. It's actually the context for that passage we saw earlier in which Eddie Corcoran makes a desperate attempt to run away from 'It'. Rather than taking us through a straightforward build-up process, it progresses in several waves of increasing tension and slight release. Before the creature's appearance, we spend a long time getting acquainted with Eddie. At this stage, there is only one (relatively low-key) reference to the supernatural – the kids who we come to know as the Losers sensed the exact moment of Eddie's death, we're told. It's enough to make us hyper-sensitive to the presence of the supernatural from that point on. But then we're immediately immersed in the boy's troubled family life and all thought of the supernatural is forgotten. This hindsight section takes the form of a sequence of violent vignettes containing some disturbing subject matter, but none of it is in any way uncanny or otherworldly.

Now the first build-up starts. The author shows us Eddie hanging around by the canal after dark. He has run away from home. It's already a worrying scenario, but, on top of that, the surroundings start to acquire a distinctly threatening feel.

> The Canal had a terrible, irresistible power in the week or two after the ice went out. He was fascinated by the way the water boiled whitely out of the cobbled arch and roared past him, bearing sticks and branches and all manner of human trash along with it. More than once he had envisioned walking beside the Canal in March with his stepdad and giving the bastard a great big motherfucking push.

As yet, the threatening quality of the natural surroundings is a reflection of the boy's anger about his abusive family life, not a reflection of any supernatural threats. But, suddenly, all that changes as a spectral hand grabs Eddie's foot. It's an apparition of his dead brother emerging from the river.

There's a short period of extreme tension as Eddie runs away, but then, just a few sentences further on, the author takes his foot off the fear gas. Eddie runs into a tree and suddenly he finds the spectre gone. In fact, he begins to question whether it was even real.

> There was the edge of the Canal, white as bone and straight as string
> in the moonlight. No sign of the thing from the Canal ... if there
> ever had been a thing.

This is the starting point for another build-up, which begins with
creepy personification but quickly becomes more menacing.

> Weeping willows draggled their thin tenebrous arms, and anything
> could be standing, slumped and insane, within their shelter.
> Eddie began to walk, trying to look everywhere at once. His
> sprained shoulder throbbed in painful sync with his heartbeat.
> Eddieeeee, the breeze moaned through the trees, don't you want to
> see meeeee, Eddieeeee? He felt flabby corpse-fingers caress the side
> of his neck. He whirled, his hands going up. As his feet tangled
> together and he fell, he saw that it had only been willow-fronds
> moving in the breeze.

The opening phrase of that quotation, 'Weeping willows draggled
their thin tenebrous arms', clearly refers to a natural phenomenon,
although it's personified as a deeply creepy, wraith-like presence.
Two short paragraphs later, we see a similar reference to the
willow, but with a rather different twist. We are told explicitly that
Eddie feels fingers on his neck, and yet ascribes that sensation to
the willow-fronds. The difference between the first reference to the
willow and this second one is simple but extremely important. In
the first, the willow is the subject of the sentence, in the second,
the fingers are the subject. With that one grammatical change, the
author gently increases the fear level. Although we probably only
register it at an unconscious level, it has the effect of solidifying
and increasing the supernatural threat.

Before bringing us face to face with 'It', the author takes us
through one more build-up cycle. He has Eddie blame the whole
thing on a bad dream.

> He got up again. He wanted to run but when he tried another
> dynamite charge went off in his shoulder and he had to stop. He
> knew somehow that he should be getting over his fright by now,
> calling himself a stupid little baby who got spooked by a reflection
> or maybe fell asleep without knowing it and had a bad dream.

But this very quickly gives way to terrifying certainty as Eddie smells rather than sees the creature pursuing him. He turns around and looks at it, finally relieving our suspense after three cycles of build-up and release. Like Georgie's view of the clown, Eddie's view of the terrifying manifestation of 'It' is not just unambiguous but positively meticulous.

> He looked behind him and saw the Creature bearing down, its white poached-egg eyes glittering, its scales dripping slime the color of seaweed, the gills up and down its bulging neck and cheeks opening and closing.

And we go on to hear all about its fishy smell, its 'batrachian hands', the 'chitinous hooks' sprouting from them and the fin on top of its 'hunched and plated head.'

Scene-level suspense of this kind – the anticipation of an impending experience of terror – is, of course, a core technique in horror fiction, and this gradual build-up from normality to a vividly violent climax is a masterclass in how to achieve it. Although the examples we've seen so far increase our uneasiness by hinting at the presence of the supernatural, for example through personification of the environment, the build-up to a terrifying moment doesn't necessarily need to reference the supernatural at all. Just about any descriptive detail can be used to increase our anxiety if it's described in such a way that it has a vaguely threatening quality. For example, when Stan comes off the phone having spoken to Mike in section 1 of Chapter 3, he disappears into the bathroom. We, like his wife, are locked out and have no idea what's happening behind the door. A powerful question is raised in our minds by the simple technique of withholding information. The author then focuses in on an unusual detail of the scene in order to amplify our curiosity to the point where it assumes menacing proportions.

> 'Stanley?' she called … the deliberate plink … pause of dripping water was her only answer.

That 'plink' is heard over and over again at regular intervals as Stan's wife repeatedly asks herself the all-important question – what is behind the bathroom door? The sound is like a form of water torture, nagging at us like the nagging question. Its sinister quality is down to a couple factors in my opinion. Firstly, it's a mundane phenomenon that the author has chosen to focus in on over a very long period, creating a feeling of preternatural significance. Secondly, it has an ice-cold unemotional quality that feels like indifference to the agitation of Stan's wife. When the bathroom door does open, the effect of the grisly scene is magnified hugely because of the atmosphere created by the dripping. This is, without doubt, one of Stephen King's subtlest suspense-building techniques.

There's another type of suspense associated with these scenes that build from normality to a violent supernatural encounter. One reason why they're so tense is that they occur at fairly widespread intervals. Chapters 1, 3 and 6 each contain one such scene (Georgie's death, Stan's death and Eddie Corcoran's death). Other supernatural incidents do occur between those incidents (Adrian Mellon's death, Ben's dream of 'It' and the viewing of George's album), but in those cases, we don't have our noses rubbed in a shocking encounter. Even Adrian Mellon's murder is not directly narrated and is presented as a subject for debate. So, the infrequency of the really tense and graphic scenes adds another dimension to the suspense of the novel. In the intervals between them, we feel a lingering dread as we look forward to the next grisly encounter with 'It'. We can't help but wonder what horrors we're going to witness next and who's going to be the victim.

The shorter-term suspense techniques we've been looking at so far are features of the early chapters of *IT*. But novels are called novels for a reason. It's because readers like novelty. As an author, you can't let your audience settle into a pattern. If you do, boredom soon takes hold. So, old techniques have to be shed and new ones constantly introduced in order to keep things interesting. Suspense-generating techniques are no exception. Accordingly, those suspenseful scenes with a violent climax cease to occur after Part 2 of the novel. As we'll see, suspense is done rather differently in the later chapters

The increasing frequency of supernatural episodes in *IT* – described in the 'Build-up' section above – is another factor that feeds into the need for different suspense-generating techniques. Unlike parts 1 and 2 of the novel, parts 4 and 5 are chock full of the supernatural. In fact, there can be several appearances of 'It' in a single chapter, as we've seen. While this serves to raise the general level of fear, you'll appreciate that it also has a tendency to rule out suspense that's based on anxious anticipation of the next supernatural encounter. If you're frequently showing the reader the source of their fear, they're less likely to feel a gnawing dread of its next appearance. Scenes in parts 4 and 5 that could have been played for suspense if they were earlier in the novel are instead played for the supernatural spectacle. The attack on Neibolt Street in Chapter 18, for example, moves very quickly from the kids entering the house to descriptions of shocking and violent phenomena because the characters already know about the bomb under the table, so to speak. In fact, they're in the process of defusing it.

However, in this new supernatural-threat-laden climate towards the end of *IT*, a completely different suspense-building technique appears and establishes dominance – namely the cliffhanger. From Chapter 19 onwards, there are many instances of this well-known structure. I'll step through the key examples for you.

Henry Bowers' attack on Eddie in the hotel is an example that I've previously mentioned. It breaks off at the end of Chapter 19, section 9.

> There was a pause, then a metallic rattle as Kaspbrak fumbled with the chain. Grinning, Henry pushed the button on the switchblade's handle. Click. He held the blade up by his cheek, ready. He heard the thumb-bolt turn. In just a moment he would plunge the blade into the skinny little creep's throat. He waited. The door opened and Eddie

We don't hear the conclusion of that sentence or see the outcome of the fight until section 11. End-of-section moments like this pile up at the end of *IT*.

There's a similar cliffhanger associated with Tom's attack on Audra. Chapter 20, section 2, ends with him grabbing her in the hotel carpark, and we don't know what has become of her until her purse is found in the tunnels in section 6. Even then, the details of her fate aren't clear.

Mike is the subject of not one but two cliffhangers. Firstly, he's very badly assaulted by Henry in the library in Chapter 19, section 3, and can't get through to the emergency services when he calls for help.

'If there's anyone there,' Mike croaked, 'a real voice behind the one I am hearing, please help me. My name is Michael Hanlon and I'm at the Derry Public Library. I am bleeding to death. If you're there, I can't hear you. I'm not being allowed to hear you. If you're there, please hurry.'

He lay on his side, drawing his legs up until he was in a fetal position. He took two turns around his right hand with the belt and concentrated on holding it as the world drifted away in those cottony, balloon-like clouds of gray.

'Hello dere, howyadoon?' Pennywise screamed from the dangling, swinging phone. 'Howyadoon, you dirty coon? Hello

It's not until Chapter 20, section 4, when Richie calls the hospital, that we hear Mike has been found and is going to survive.

Mike also comes under threat as he lies in the hospital recovering. Chapter 21, section 10, ends with the following chilling lines.

He walked into the room, and as he stood at the foot of the bed, Mike saw with a hopeless chill how blank Mark Lamonica's eyes were. His head was slightly cocked, as if hearing distant music. He took his hand out of his pocket. There was a syringe in it.

'This will put you to sleep,' Mark said, and began to walk toward the bed.

We have to wait until section 12 to see him fight off the attacker.

Around the same time, the author creates a cliffhanger in relation to one of the appearances of 'It'. Chapter 21, section 7, ends as follows.

Bill listened. He heard dragging, shambling footsteps approaching them in the dark … and he was afraid.

'A-A-Audra?' he called … and knew already that it was not her.

Whatever was shambling toward them drew closer.

Bill struck a light.

Only in section 9 do we see what's shambling towards them. Bill's flaring match reveals 'It' in the form of Georgie.

Each example uses the closing lines of a section to pose a clear question about something we're emotionally engaged with. That's important – it's the pre-existing emotion that makes us desperately want closure. Usually, the question is about personal safety. We just have to know whether Eddie or Mike will survive, for example, because we've come to know them and like them. But sometimes the question stimulates other forms of curiosity. In the last example, we're compelled to wonder what's out there in the darkness of the tunnel.

You will also have noticed that the interval between the question and answer parts of the cliffhanger varies. Some kind of diversion into another subject is obligatory once the cliffhanger question has been posed, but often it's for no more than one scene. However, there's no reason why the diversion shouldn't be longer. In one case, the interval is so large that another cliffhanger is created and resolved before it concludes. (Overlapping cliffhangers means double the suspense!) It's important to note, though, that the long interval is only possible in this case because Mike is not engaged in the main action of the story. In other words, the 'inner cliffhanger' is best drawn from secondary action or subplots.

In my view, these cliffhangers, arriving late on the scene, bring a dramatic edge to the suspense that the other techniques lack. That's because of the extreme specificity of the question posed by a cliffhanger – our attention is focused in on one piece of information that's limited in nature but of great importance to how the story proceeds.

Style

Creating fear in a horror novel is not just about large-scale structures and grand ideas about metaphysical content. It also depends on sentence-level writing style. We've already seen that detailed attention to wording is essential in creating effects at the scene level, but I'd like to point out a couple of writing techniques that diffuse a chilling atmosphere through the novel as a whole.

A Haunted Text

When I first read *IT*, many years ago, I remember noticing repeated uses of the word 'float'. As you'll no doubt recall, it's a word that's closely linked to the supernatural aspects of the novel. It's often crooned to the victims of 'It' just before they meet a ghastly end. However, quite a few of the 116 uses of the word occur in non-horrific contexts. At first, I thought it might be a coincidence, but eventually I had to conclude that the author was deliberately dropping the word 'float' into the text. In my opinion, it gives the text a disturbing quality that's rather like seeing eerie shadows and sudden movements out of the corner of your eye.

This approach to the cultivation of fear in the reader is quite different from some of the other techniques that we've discussed in this chapter. For one thing, it's more about creating a nagging sense of unease rather than delivering a shiver of actual fear. It's also about maintaining a sense of mystery rather than bringing the reader face to face with scary things. Compare this with the technique discussed above in which a steady flow of metaphysical details gives the reader a more and more complete understanding of the supernatural. That has a tendency to gradually drive away shadows. To avoid either dispelling the reader's fear by showing too much or, on the other hand, frustrating the reader by dwelling too much on shadow and uncertainty, it's wise to pursue a variety of techniques, including some that reveal and some that conceal. That's precisely what we see in *IT*.

Let's look a little more closely at the repetition of the word 'float'. The first thing to notice is that quite a lot of effort goes into establishing the special status and meaning of the word early in the novel. In just the third section of Chapter 1, the word 'float' is repeated 8 times by Pennywise. The literal meaning of those uses is clear – they refer to the bodies of the creature's victims floating down in the sewers under Derry. But there's also a rich metaphorical quality to the word that's brewed, distilled and intensified through repetition at a moment of extreme horror. In this way it acquires the power to radiate a sense of menace.

Another effect of the early repetition of 'float' is to sensitise readers to the word. As a result, we begin to notice uses of it in other contexts – not just occasions when it's spoken by 'It' or used to describe one of the creature's manifestations. For example, we notice it in a description of the limo driven by Eddie as he heads for Derry.

Eddie floats the big car along

In this context, the word 'float' is not ostensibly linked to 'It' in any way, and yet it still manages to produce a vague sense of threat because of its strong associations with the creature.

As the story develops, some of these apparently innocuous

occurrences have a slightly stronger connection with 'It' – for example when Mr Nell, the police officer, breaks up the dam-building party and gives the kids a telling off, referring to 'Bar'ns playing amongst the floating turdies'. But plenty of others have no clear connection, and they still give the reader a chill when thy appear.

Repeated use of the word 'float' is just one way in which the author suffuses his text with the unseen presence of 'It'. There are many other examples of imagery with supernatural associations popping up in apparently innocuous settings. In Chapter 4, section 2, for example, Ben's mortification at being mocked by bullies – especially in front of girls – is described.

> If a hole leading into the underworld had opened before him at that very moment, Ben would have dropped into it without a sound

In most other contexts, the idea of dropping through a hole into the underworld would be just a figure of speech – a totally innocent way of describing intense embarrassment. But, coming only a few chapters after we have seen a small boy being dragged down into the sewer, it has an eerie, resonant quality.

Gallows Humour

Strange as it may seem, *IT* has a vein of black humour running through it – a scattering of observations that induce laughter at the most horrific of moments. Instinctively, you would imagine that humour is the enemy of fear. Laughter is usually associated with relaxation and being comfortable in your surroundings, whereas fear is associated with the fight or flight reflex – a state of extreme tension and preparedness for danger. So, how do we explain, for example, the brief description in Chapter 1, section 4, of the dead chicken that bobbed alongside Georgie's paper boat for a while as it drifted through the sewer?

> For a while it ran neck-and-neck with a dead chicken that floated with its yellowy, reptilian toes pointed at the dripping ceiling

What could be more inappropriate in the immediate aftermath of Georgie's grisly death?

Another example of dark humour – equally difficult to explain –

is the observation in Chapter 8, section 4, that Richie's jacket 'parted down the back with a loud ripping noise that sounded weirdly like a big fart.' This in the middle of a desperate scramble to escape from a werewolf. One might conceivably argue that the fart joke reflects Richie's anarchic mind at a moment when he's the viewpoint character.

But I have another theory that may go some way to explaining both these instances of laughter at horrific moments. Have you ever eaten a strawberry with a little bit of black pepper? It seems like an odd combination, because the two flavours are so different, but many people who try it agree that the heat of the spice enhances the fruit flavours of the strawberry. Just so with humour in horror novels. Used in tiny pinches, it can actually give the reader an extra shiver at a moment of extreme horror – particularly if it has a certain blackness to it, like the chicken with its toes pointing upwards.

Takeaway

- A horror novel's primary purpose is to induce fear in the reader.
  - Content
    - Anxiety
      - Horror fiction should exploit deep-seated fears about the reliability of things that you normally trust or hold dear.
    - The Chase
      - If you examine your dream life you will find that the unconscious mind is a reservoir of images that give form to our fears.
    - Metaphysics
      - A consistent explanation for the presence of the supernatural or the uncanny is essential.
      - Nothing is new in the metaphysics of horror, so raid sources from the past.
      - Gradually increase the scope of the metaphysics in your fictional

universe.
- Keep the drip of metaphysical information coming.

o Structures
- Build-up
  - The number of encounters with the novel's 'big evil' should increase.
  - Later chapters should contain more direct encounters.
  - The direct encounters become more extended – the climax is ultra-extended.
  - A group of shorter encounters may precede the climax of the novel.
- Suspense
  - Suspense for the long term
    o Early on, maximise our sense of the negative situation afflicting the main characters.
    o Also early on, establish the goal that will save the main characters from their affliction.
  - Suspense for the shorter term
    o Begin scenes that involve a direct manifestation of the supernatural with normal human events.
    o Introduce details that might be supernatural but might not.
    o Reveal the supernatural with full, vivid description.
    o Keep changing the means of creating suspense – *IT* uses cliffhangers in the later chapters.

o Style
- A haunted text
  - Encourage the reader to associate

certain vocabulary with the supernatural then drop that vocabulary into innocent contexts.

- Gallows humour
  - A laugh at moments of extreme horror can enhance the experience.

2. THEMATIC LAYERS

'There were other things, things he hadn't thought of in years, trembling just below the surface.'
– Stephen King, *IT*

I've argued that the primary duty of a horror novelist is to terrify. But a great story never functions on just one level. If it were exclusively about generating fear, the experience would be extreme at the time, but quickly fade from memory. What readers really crave – and what leaves them thinking about a novel for months, if not years after they put it down – is a feeling of having gone through a profound experience rather than just a terrifying one. To achieve that, the story needs to contain many different thematic layers of meaning.

That word 'theme' can be quite difficult to pin down. Another way of describing what I'm referring to would be 'threads of connection between the story and real life.' We're all accustomed to the idea of stories having a 'moral' – a concise statement of the lesson that one can take away from its events. That's a crude manifestation of theme. In a complex modern narrative like *IT*, theme is rather more complex and ambiguous, but it's still basically an argument for viewing some aspect of the world in a certain way.

Naturally, these layers of meaning or theme shouldn't intrude into the story's events in an unsubtle or distracting way. A skilful author will find indirect ways of weaving them through the fabric of the story – for example, through the use of metaphor. As we will see, though, one can be more direct in the statement of theme towards the end of a story. In fact, that's one of the hallmarks of a well-structured tale. But, at all points throughout a novel, it is vital that the reader never feels the author is pressing opinions on them. This will only make them feel patronised.

It's also necessary to ensure that there's coherence and connection between the layers. It's one of the most challenging aspects of novel writing, but when it happens – through hard work or serendipity – it provides a wonderful 'yeah-it-all-makes-sense' feeling. That's what you're aiming to achieve. In the context of a horror novel, there must always be a strong connection between the layers of meaning and the nature of fear – specifically, the kind of fears that the author has chosen to evoke with the main plot of the novel. Let's look at how Stephen King does that in *IT*, taking the layers of meaning one at a time.

Social Themes

The idea that there is something generally wrong with the fabric of society in Derry is central to the novel. The supernatural evil that haunts the city – the novel's chief source of fear – is used again and again as a tool for highlighting the human wickedness that characterises human societies. In fact, the sheer terror generated by the supernatural amplifies the author's denunciation of social evils. A single technique allows the author to use his horror novel as a means of delivering social commentary: he constantly blurs the distinction between human evil and supernatural evil.

Let's start by taking a look at the festival described in Chapter 2. The events that are described – homophobic bullying followed by a murder at the hands of Pennywise – are atypical for the novel. The victim is not a child, members of the Losers' Club are not involved in any way and the sections are short, moving around from person to person. If I'd been the publisher's editor, I would have been tempted to cut it completely. However, it does serve an important purpose: it gives us a snapshot of Derry society as a whole – an entire city at play as represented by a cast of around 10 characters.

And what do we learn about Derry? Most obviously, we learn that it has a vein of homophobic hatred running through it. The action begins with Don Hagarty speaking to police about events leading up to the death of his friend Adrian Mellon. They are both gay men. A group of thugs had been outraged by Mellon's camp appearance and decided to teach him a lesson. But this attitude is not restricted to the thugs – towards the beginning of the chapter, we view the events through the eyes of a cop, and his attitude is dripping with disdain for the victim and his friend.

> This man – if you want to call him a man – was wearing lipstick and satin pants so tight you could almost read the wrinkles in his cock. Grief or no grief, pain or no pain, he was, after all, just a queer. Like his friend, the late Adrian Mellon.

Moreover, the graffiti at a certain spot in Derry reveals troubling levels of hate in the city as a whole. It makes Hagarty want to leave the place altogether.

> 'Whoever writes these little homilies has got a case of the deep-down crazies. I'd feel better if I thought it was just one person, one isolated sickie, but …' Don swept his arm vaguely down the length of the Kissing Bridge. 'There's a lot of this stuff … and I just don't think one person did it all. That's why I want to leave Derry, Ade. Too many places and too many people seem to have the deep-down crazies.'

When it comes to the murder of Adrian Mellon, Hagarty once again tries to express a feeling that there is something evil about Derry as a whole. Except that, given the involvement of the clown in the murder, there is now also a supernatural side to Hagarty's insight. Derry is wrong on some level beyond the human, in his view.

> 'I started after him … and the clown looked back. I saw its eyes, and all at once I understood who it was.'
> 'Who was it, Don?' Harold Gardener asked softly.
> 'It was Derry,' Don Hagarty said. 'It was this town.'

Hagarty saw with his own two eyes the clown dragging Adrian off to kill him, and yet he identifies the killer as Derry itself. This is a fascinating statement. It seems to suggest that the clown is in some way identical with Derry – that, although the clown did the killing, it was only expressing the same evil as the thugs who chased after them.

This is just the first example of the blurring of supernatural and human evil in *IT*. The author uses more than one technique to achieve this effect, but most often it happens in a way that's similar to the account of Adrian Mellon's murder – an act of human evil is taking place and 'It' steps into the scene to participate. The historical anecdotes reported by Mike the librarian in his interlude sections are mostly examples of this. For example, in the Second Interlude, we hear how some black soldiers are at a dance in 1930 when the building is deliberately set on fire. As the people inside are suffering and dying horribly, we are told that a large bird, held aloft by balloons, was seen. There's no clear explanation for this phenomenon, which happens over and over again, both in Mike's historical anecdotes and in the novel's main narrative. Maybe 'It' is driving the evil. Maybe the creature is just drawn to human wickedness. Or maybe it's brought into being by human minds engaged in hatred and violence. The author keeps it vague for a reason – he wants to blur the distinction between human evil and supernatural evil as much as possible.

In other scenes and subplots, there's a slightly different dynamic between human evil and the supernatural. Certain characters begin explicitly cooperating with 'It' after a period when they were apparently acting out ordinary human evil. It's never made clear whether their Mephistophelean pact with supernatural evil was freely chosen, or whether their evil lives made them easy targets for supernatural control, or, indeed, whether they were actually influenced by the supernatural from the word go. The result is, once again, a blurring of the human and the supernatural. For example, some of the members of the Losers' Club were bullied as kids. Their tormentor, Henry Bowers, is later targeted by 'It', becomes the creature's puppet and goes after the Losers, intent on murder. Where does his innate human badness end and the supernatural influence of 'It' begin? It's impossible to say. And, as if there weren't enough uncertainty, another dimension is added by the fact that Henry Bowers is in a mental health facility when he starts to hear the voice of 'It'. Does his condition leave him vulnerable to evil influences or result from a life of evil? We are not told.

Yet another technique is used throughout the novel to blur human and supernatural evil. It's connected with the fact that Derry society seems unable to see evil that's happening right under its nose. Again and again, individual characters seem to overlook or ignore dreadful events going on in front of them. In Chapter 19, section 2, for example, Bev is running from her father in obvious distress, but her plight makes no impression on the people around her. It's so extreme a phenomenon that we're tempted to think the onlookers are in some way blinded by 'It'. But there's never any confirmation of that. It's equally possible that it's due to a human failing.

The thematic purpose of these techniques is, of course, to shine a light on evil human behaviours in the real world – racism, child abuse, antisemitism, bullying and so on. In fact, there's a broad range of social ills that Stephen King calls out and implicitly condemns in *IT*. Many other horror novels use similar techniques to focus on a specific evil. But King is more concerned with a general rottenness that can afflict a society as a whole. The supernatural element of the novel is his metaphor for that rottenness. The shape-shifting quality of 'It' is well-suited to that metaphorical role. Other writers have shaped the 'big evil' element of their story to reflect a more specific social evil. For example, the monster in *Frankenstein* is a metaphor for the creative imagination that can't be controlled and may ultimately destroy you. So, its characteristics are tailored specifically to that metaphorical role.

But there's a danger inherent in using the supernatural or some other 'big evil' as a metaphor for commenting on social evil. It's possible that the novel will end up downplaying the reality of human evil. That's the last thing you want to do if one of your thematic goals is to condemn certain evil human behaviours that shape society. The need to keep human moral agency in the spotlight is, I believe, another reason why Stephen King goes to some lengths to blur the distinction between human evil and supernatural evil. The ambiguity ensures that, for most of the novel, 'It' feels like a metaphor as well as a character. Only late on in the novel, with the passages that give us the creature's internal monologue, do we become exclusively aware of it as a rounded character.

There's another technique used by the author to highlight social evil that needs to be mentioned. In a sense, it's the opposite of the blurring discussed above. Rather than creating uncertainty around evil, this technique seeks to draw our attention to the nature of evil by providing contrasting characters. In addition to showing us scenes of depravity and violence, the novel gives us a few scattered examples of human decency. I'm not referring to the near-superhuman goodness of those involved in attacking 'It' head on. I'm referring to characters whose lives of ordinary goodness contradict the human evil of Derry (and to some extent the supernatural evil oppressing the city). Just as a point of light can make the darkness around it seem all the darker, so also, the effect of these decent characters is actually to accentuate the horrifying nature of evil.

The best example of this is Mike Hanlon. I suppose it's only to be expected that a writer's ultimate example of human decency would be a librarian. But Stephen King also imbues this profession with an almost priest-like status. The book that he's working on, which is quoted at length in the interludes, is like Derry's communal memory. It's a contradiction of the city's blindness to evil, which I discussed above. Although Mike is the character who galvanises the other Losers into action by calling them, he doesn't go down into the tunnels to confront evil directly. His role is to be a contrast and a counterweight to evil.

Mike is not quite the only character in this category. There's a small number of others. For example, in Chapter 4, section 6, we see Ben's mother giving him a lecture on not staying out too late. She has seen the crimes going on in Derry and taken them to heart. We also get to meet Mike's parents in Chapter 6, section 5. They 're in the habit of hugging their child and fostering his curiosity – quite the opposite of other Derry residents' indifference to the welfare of children. In fact, they make it clear that they disapprove of a local police chief who glorifies brutal aspects of the city's history. Significantly, the Hanlons live a hard-working but happy rural existence. They're not immersed in Derry society or the evil that pervades it.

Psychological Themes

Now let's consider the layer of psychological meaning in *IT*. In overview, the novel uses the supernatural as a source of metaphors that illuminate issues of psychological trauma in childhood, showing how those traumas affect a person later in life. Each of the novel's main characters is enduring some form of long-term psychological suffering, and, as you would expect, the causes of their suffering have strong connections with the subject of fear.

Chapter 3 is the section of the novel during which the psychological layer is set up. The author spends the whole chapter establishing understanding and sympathy for the particular types of mental suffering experienced by the novel's main characters. It's a gigantic exercise in exposition. The initial stimulus is a call to each of the characters from Mike Hanlon, announcing that 'It' has returned. Immediately after each call, information about the recipient's childhood trauma begins to emerge. This happens in a variety of ways, but the most successful sequences are those that obey the oft-quoted rule of description, 'Show don't tell.'

As an example of good psychological exposition, let's consider the events around Bev's call from Mike in Chapter 3, section 5. The first and most obvious way in which the text shows (rather than tells) the nature of Bev's psychological problem is by adopting her husband Tom as the viewpoint character. Effectively, Bev is confined to the prison of Tom's perceptions.

In addition to simply squeezing Bev out of the viewpoint position, Tom's viewpoint is narrated with an extremely obnoxious voice. It rubs our noses in the truly unlikable sentiments he expresses. As a result, his character quickly becomes oppressive.

> ... oh, looky here, friends and neighbors! Oh you just looky right here! Is she taking a suitcase out of the closet? A suitcase? By God, she is!

This oppressiveness makes us more inclined to see alternative truths beneath Tom's perceptions. He has a predatory view of Bev as someone he can easily dominate. But, ironically, the details he interprets as signs of weakness make a different impression on the reader. They come across as a sad physical testimony of her psychological suffering.

> ... she was weak ... weak somehow. It was as if she was sending out radio signals which only he could receive. You could point to certain things – how much she smoked (but he had almost cured her of that), the restless way her eyes moved, never quite meeting the eyes of whoever was talking to her, only touching them from time to time and then leaping nimbly away; her habit of lightly rubbing her elbows when she was nervous; the look of her fingernails, which were kept neat but brutally short. Tom noticed this latter the first time he met her. She picked up her glass of white wine, he saw her

nails, and thought: She keeps them short like that because she bites them.

Later, Bev breaks out of the prison of Tom's viewpoint. We start to see things through her eyes.

> He thought she would run. Probably for the bathroom. Maybe for the stairs. Instead, she stood her ground.
>
> ...
>
> Now she was crying, her breath coming in high, screamy sobs. Time after time she had seen herself leaving him, leaving Tom's tyranny as she had left that of her father, stealing away in the night, bags piled in the trunk of her Cutlass. She was not a stupid woman ...

The first part of the quotation is clearly Tom's viewpoint. The second part is clearly Bev's. This comes at the precise moment of her physical rebellion against her husband.

We have no idea what it is that made Bev vulnerable to a controlling creep like Tom for so long, but the details that we're shown through Bev's viewpoint give some very strong clues.

> And just who was this caveman in the bloody undershorts, anyway? Her husband? Her father?

The outlines of a trauma connected with her father are beginning to emerge. And soon, the narration of Bev's viewpoint reveals that there's a sexual element as well.

> Oh hey, look at this – Beverly got another parking ticket. One with the belt ... across the breasts. He was good. He rarely bruised. It didn't even hurt that much. Except for the humiliation. That hurt. And what hurt worse was knowing that part of her craved the hurt. Craved the humiliation.

This bravura example of showing rather than telling is some of the best material in the psychological layer of the novel. It reveals the wounds at the heart of a character's soul by showing the consequences rather than giving an account of the original trauma or referring directly to it any way.

Supernatural evil is an extremely flexible tool. In the hands of a skilled author, it is a rich source of metaphorical images that can be used to home in on all sorts of issues and explore them more deeply. But because the horror genre is primarily about pushing mental buttons that give readers an experience of fear, it's a superb vehicle for exploring dark psychological waters. And psychological states like Bev's are certainly dark. Once her inner trauma – and that of all the other main characters – has been set up in Chapter 3, the author begins using manifestations of supernatural evil to deepen our understanding of those psychological states.

There's rather a diverse selection of imagery associated with supernatural apparitions in *IT*. By contrast, many horror novels choose to give evil a single face, typically revealing it in small steps. Stephen King's imagery of the supernatural is like a lexicon of ghostly manifestations from literature, at least in this novel. In other novels – the vampire novel *Salem's Lot* for example – the imagery is more focused. However, both approaches are equally suitable for exploring psychological territory. The key technique used by Stephen King throughout his body of work is to shape each manifestation of supernatural evil so that it functions as a powerful metaphor for psychological suffering.

For example, in Chapter 5 of *IT*, Bev is terrified by the sight of blood gushing from the plughole of a bathroom sink, accompanied by taunting voices from the drain. It's an image that powerfully dramatises the abusive nature of her relationship with her father during puberty. And, thanks to the psychological set-up in Chapter 3, the reader very quickly picks up on the metaphorical content of the supernatural episode. The sexual trauma that was hinted at in the fight with her husband in Chapter 3 is now laid bare, clarified and intensified by the bloody apparition.

> There was blood … blood everywhere … and her father didn't see it.
> 'Daddy –' She had no idea what might have come next, but her father interrupted her.
> 'I worry about you,' Al Marsh said. 'I don't think you're ever going to grow up, Beverly. You go out running around, you don't do hardly any of the housework around here, you can't cook, you can't sew. Half the time you're off on a cloud someplace with your nose stuck in a book and the other half you've got vapors and megrims. I worry.'
> His hand suddenly swung and spatted painfully against her buttocks.
> …
> 'I worry a lot,' he said

...
'An awful lot,' he said, and punched her in the stomach.

This passage describes the supernatural episode in such a way that
we are in no doubt about the nature of Bev's trauma and her
father's involvement in it. We're told that he's in the habit of
punishing her for all sorts of behaviours, which he blames on
mood changes associated with menstruation – that's presumably
what he means by 'vapors and megrims'. However, his slaps and
punches clearly show that a sexual interest in his daughter is at the
heart of all this. The resulting terror and guilt experienced by Bev is
expressed by the desperate struggle to remove stains from the
bathroom after an eruption of blood from the plughole.

IT contains other examples of supernatural ordeals that express
the unique psychological suffering of a character. Bill, for example,
sees 'It' emerging from his dead brother's photo album – a
poignant expression of his feelings of guilt over Georgie's death.

With some of the main characters, supernatural struggle is used
as a way of exploring solutions to psychological trauma. With
Eddie, for example, his problem is a mother who constantly
imagines that he's sick or in danger. She persuaded him that he
absolutely needs an aspirator, and yet the aspirator contains
nothing more than water. Although initially angry that the
pharmacist has pulled the wool over his eyes by supplying a
placebo year after year, Eddie learns a valuable lesson: that the
imagination can be a powerful self-help tool as well as a source of
terrors. Accordingly, the inhaler becomes a feature of the boy's
struggle with supernatural evil.

> He raised the aspirator
> (acid it's acid if I want it to be so eat it eat it eat)
> 'BATTERY ACID, FUCKNUTS!' Eddie screamed
> ...
> He felt tentacles touch him, but tentatively. He triggered the
> aspirator again, coating the Eye, and felt/heard that mewling again
> ... now a hurt, surprised sound.

The aspirator has been transformed into a metaphor for the
psychological truth learned by Eddie. Its squirts of water inflict
pain on the ghastly giant eyeball, just like a thought that may be a
product of the imagination but nevertheless drives away

psychological problems.

If a piece of horror fiction uses a single supernatural phenomenon as a metaphor for multiple forms psychological suffering, there will be an expectation among readers that the supernatural phenomenon should express a deep psychological truth underlying all the aspects of psychological trauma and healing alluded to in the story. This is certainly something that we see in *IT*.

Let's consider two passages from the novel that fulfil this role of unifying and explaining all the forms of psychological suffering in the novel. Firstly, an episode from Chapter 21, section 6, when the kids are making their way through the tunnels under Derry. After a number of misadventures in the tunnels, they come across a little door.

> There was a mark on the door, and heaped at its foot was a pile of bones. Small bones. The bones of God alone knew how many children. They had come to the place of It. The mark on the door, then: what was that?
> Bill marked it as a paper boat.
> Stan saw it as a bird rising toward the sky – a phoenix, perhaps.
> Michael saw a hooded face – that of crazy Butch Bowers, perhaps, if it could only be seen.
> Richie saw two eyes behind a pair of spectacles.
> Beverly saw a hand doubled up into a fist.
> Eddie believed it to be the face of the leper
> …
> It swung open on a flood of sick yellow-green light. That zoo smell wafted out at them, incredibly strong, incredibly potent now. One by one they passed through the fairytale door, and into the lair of It.

This image of the little door and its strange marking is almost allegorical in its clarity of meaning. It communicates the idea that the psychological sufferings of each member of the Losers' Club, different as they are from one another, have a common explanation. Just as 'It' is the single evil behind the multiple meanings of the symbol on the door, so also there must be a single principle of evil behind all the childhood traumas of the Losers.

However, it's interesting to note that, when we do encounter 'It' behind the door, the author actually retreats from clarity. He seems determined, instead, to convey the transcendent nature of whatever 'It' represents. It's certainly difficult to pin down what the 'deadlights' experience means on a psychological level, or any other level. Intensity of action is a feature of the closing chapters of most genre novels – one of the most important ingredients in our enjoyment of popular fiction, in fact. So, it seems that, in Stephen King's view, giving the reader an intense concluding experience is more important than revealing a core truth behind psychological suffering, even if you've been building up to that insight for some time. One could argue that, if you haven't given the reader a reasonably good idea of the truths at the heart of your novel before the final showdown, you've probably misjudged the on-going metaphorical content. In *IT*, there are certainly plenty of moments when we become aware of what the creature stands for, psychologically speaking, and how that explains all of the traumas of the characters.

So what exactly does the creature represent when viewed as a psychological metaphor? My second passage is much clearer on that than the first. In Chapter 10, the Losers' Club gets together for the first time since childhood. They meet in a Chinese restaurant in Derry and discuss what's been happening in their lives. One by one, they open up about the traumas that have affected them since childhood – their unique and personal circumstances. But then the conversation takes a significant turn. Encouraged by Mike, they start to look for commonality of experience. He first probes their obvious career success as a group.

> Mike nodded. 'Things are out of order with your own lives, too, you know. None of you left Derry untouched … without Its mark on you. All of you forgot what happened here, and your memories of that summer are still only fragmentary. And then there's the passingly curious fact that you're all rich.'
> Next, Mike draws attention to their childlessness as a group.
> 'I have a feeling that Stan, with his ordered mind, might have had some idea.'
> 'Maybe he did,' Beverly said. 'Maybe that's why he killed himself. Maybe he understood that if there was magic, it wouldn't work for grownups.'
> 'I think it could, though,' Mike said. 'Because there's one other thing we six have in common. I wonder if any of you have realized what that is.' It was Bill's turn to open his mouth and then shut it again.
> 'Go on,' Mike said. 'You know what it is. I can see it on your face.'
> 'I'm not sure I know,' Bill replied, 'but I think w-we're all childless.

Is that ih-it?' There was a moment of shocked silence. 'Yeah,' Mike said. 'That's it.'

This powerful scene draws out common supernatural influences on the suffering of all the Losers. Specifically, their career success is ascribed to the simple act of getting away from 'It', but also to the weird forgetfulness that set in after 1958. In addition, their childlessness is blamed on the fact that the creature fears the power of the young. For the purposes of the current discussion, the most important aspect of these shared supernatural influences is the way they suggest a parallel psychological account of evil at work in the lives of the Losers: each of them has left behind a traumatic upbringing and tried to deal with hurtful memories through repression and hard work. Then, only a few paragraphs further on, the author takes us right to the heart of that shared psychological condition. As the group members open their fortune cookies, a tidal wave of apparitions assaults them. This is the moment when, for the first time in the novel, they openly discuss the fact that 'It' can extract painful images from their minds and use them to inspire fear. It would take a particularly insensitive reader to miss the metaphorical significance of this: 'It' is fear itself. Fear is the factor that underlies all their sufferings. This is the moment when Stephen King completes the important task of providing a single psychological account of evil corresponding to the single source of supernatural evil.

In case you haven't noticed it, I'd also like to point out that the reunion – that moment of deep insight into one of the novel's layers of meaning – occurs exactly at the midpoint of the novel. In most forms of popular storytelling – movies and popular fiction especially – the midpoint is a moment when we acquire some major insight through important plot developments. It's so common to structure stories like this that we've become ultra-sensitive to the thematic lessons that an author chooses to convey there.

Perhaps the climax of the novel fails to clarify the creature's meaning as a psychological metaphor because the job has already been done at the midpoint – that powerful fulcrum of the plot. I can see how this would be desirable from a dramatic perspective, since it allows the final chapters to be given over to tense action. This is an important lesson: a writer needs to learn which moments are most appropriate for focusing on particular types of thematic material.

Artistic Themes

One of the threads that runs through Stephen King's extremely varied output is the presence of characters who are authors. Sure enough, *IT* contains not just an author but a horror novelist, namely Bill Denbrough. In fact, Bill just happens to have written a book that sounds very much like *IT*, as we learn in Chapter 3.

> The film version of The Black Rapids is called Pit of the Black Demon

This is an enormous clue – a hint that one of Stephen King's objectives in *IT* is to reflect on the nature and meaning of horror fiction. Personally, I think including a layer in your novel that explores the meaning of novel writing or artistic creation in general is ill-advised. It runs the risk of looking self-indulgent unless you have a really masterful touch. Needless to say, Stephen King pulls it off in style. He uses a number of different techniques to tackle the subject.

Firstly, we receive one or two direct insights into the significance of writing in the life of Bill the novelist. This example comes from Bill's childhood. It refers to the typewriter that he wrote on as a kid.

> His folks had given it to him for Christmas two years ago, and Bill sometimes wrote stories on it. He did this a bit more frequently since George's death. The pretending seemed to ease his mind.

The suggestion is that we should see novel writing as yet another symptom of trauma, or a coping strategy – at least in Bill's case. As you'll no doubt have recognised, this is a moment of cross-fertilisation with the psychological thematic layer, which also revolves around the trauma experienced by the Losers. Interconnections between layers of a novel are always welcome. In fact, the more richly interconnected they are, the better.

The second technique that I want to mention is related to the nature of 'It'. As we saw in the discussion metaphysics, one of the creature's key characteristics is the fact that it plunders the imaginations of its victims in order to terrify them. In fact, it particularly craves the imaginings of children, consuming them like a delicious foodstuff. This is exactly how a horror novel or horror movie uses terrifying imagery to scare us. It raids our unconscious for images that touch on deep fears, then it amplifies those images and plays them back to us. In essence, 'It' is a personification of the horror genre itself.

A third technique used to comment on the nature of horror fiction is the inclusion of other 'horror-like' stories within the plot – stories that are told by various characters or sometimes simply mentioned in passing. The most common of these is the story of 'The Three Billy Goats Gruff'. It appears again and again. For example, a librarian is reading it to some children when Ben visits the library as a kid in Chapter 4, section 6. Then, in Chapter 11, section 1, a librarian of a later generation is once again reading 'The Three Billy Goats Gruff'. And there are other mentions of the story. The inclusion of this story at several points in the novel releases a whole host of insights into the nature of the horror genre. What it comes down to is that 'The Three Billy Goats Gruff' is the most basic version of the type of horror story that Stephen King has given us in *IT*. Both are about a monster hiding underground, waiting to consume the unwary. Moreover, *IT* has multiple heroes and a repetitive plot structure that echoes 'The Three Billy Goats Gruff'. Instead of three goat heroes encountering a monster in three consecutive episodes, it has six human heroes who encounter their enemy in childhood and adulthood – but the basic principle of multiple heroes and encounters is the same.

Another important point about 'The Three Billy Goats Gruff' is that it's a story aimed at children. This is clearly noteworthy, given that *IT* revolves around childhood experiences and their long-term effects. Stephen King seems particularly interested in the special affinity children (or the children inside adults) have for stories that revolve around a conflict with a monstrous enemy. During Ben's visit to the library in Chapter 4, the narration comments on the way the children totally engage with the fairy tale being read to them.

Miss Davies spoke in the low, growling tones of the troll in the story. Some of the little ones covered their mouths and giggled, but most only watched her solemnly, accepting the voice of the troll as they accepted the voices of their dreams, and their grave eyes reflected the eternal fascination of the fairytale: would the monster be bested ... or would it feed?

I can't help but think that this total engagement with the fairy tale is a faint echo of Georgie's terror at the thought of going down into a cellar populated by imaginary monsters, mentioned in Chapter 1. The implication is that, 'The Three Billy Goats Gruff' and horror stories in general, achieve a hold over their audience by closely reflecting their unconscious fears. And, by the way, the suggestion that stories can get as close to you as your nightmares should have your alarm bells ringing, since it is, without doubt, creating a link between horror fiction and 'It'. Both raid the imaginations of children in order to terrify them. It's another example of rich interconnection between layers of the novel.

'The Three Bill Goats Gruff' is a relatively benign exemplar a story that draws on the unconscious in order to establish a hold over the audience. Other stories that appear in the pages of *IT* make a much more terrifying impression on the characters and readers alike. A key example is the werewolf movie that Richie, Ben and Bev go to see in Chapter 8, section 6. In this case, the story is of interest to us because it apparently appeals so strongly to a movie theatre full of pubescent kids (and to the teenager inside all of us). The mild sexual tension between the two boys and Bev before and during their movie 'date' encourages us to see the werewolf movie as a reflection of unconscious fears about becoming an adult. In this case, the author lays bare the similarity between movies that feed off unconscious fear and the way 'It' operates, because, before too long, we see Richie encountering the monster in the form of a werewolf at Neibolt Street – the creature has raided his mind. There truly is a tight knot of imagery connecting the artistic and psychological themes of the novel with its metaphysical content. This density of meaning is what horror novelists should be aiming for.

We now move on to a fourth technique used in *IT* to explore the nature and meaning of horror fiction. It involves giving certain characters a unique insight into the events going on around them. In fact, their perspective verges on actual awareness of being in a horror story. Mike is the most obvious example. His interludes are lighthouse moments of reflection on the meaning of the various apparitions of 'It' – their social and psychological significance. At one point in the Second Interlude, his insights actually seem to take on the tone of a literary critic speculating about the function of horror fiction. He's relating his father's account of the deaths of African-American soldier in the '30s and chooses to include his father's insight into the importance of telling horrific stories.

> 'This story goan give you nightmares, Mikey?'
> I opened my mouth to lie, and then thought better of it. And I think now that if I had lied, he would have stopped right there. He was far gone by then, but maybe not that far gone.
> 'I guess so,' I said.
> 'That's not such a bad thing,' he said to me. 'In nightmares we can think the worst. That's what they're for, I guess.'

Although that final statement isn't referring directly to the novel *IT*, it might as well be. It presents us, once again, with a link between the psychology of trauma and the meaning of horror narratives – they are stories that mimic the way our unconscious mind processes fear.

Mike isn't the only character who almost seems aware of being in a horror novel. Ben, Bill and even 'It' all have moments when they could be critiquing the novel around them as they comment on the nature of imagination – specifically its twin roles in creating and quelling fear. The boldest example occurs in the Epilogue. Bill senses that his life story is in some way drawing to a conclusion, or at least coming full circle, and he chooses to describe that in terms of a novel.

> We are leaving Derry, and if this was a story it would be the last half-dozen pages or so; get ready to put this one up on the shelf and forget it.

The danger with these techniques that draw attention to the fictionality of the novel you're reading is that they can break the illusion for the reader. So, it's interesting to note that Stephen King leaves the most glaring use of such a technique until nearly the end of the novel, after the climax of the action, when we're withdrawing from the story. In fact, rather cleverly, that quote from Bill draws attention to this withdrawal of the imagination that occurs towards the end of a story. He uses it as a metaphor for the way we leave childhood fears behind.

Political Themes

Right from the start of *IT*, political dimensions of fear are hinted at.

In the second section of Chapter 1, we hear about the fears of a small boy – Georgie. Like all children, he has a litany of things that scare him, and, as one would expect, the list includes monsters in dark places. But he's also aware of more grounded kinds of bogeymen – namely 'Commies' and murderers. He may not experience them directly or even grasp why they should be feared, but they're certainly lodged in his consciousness.

> Every now and then someone went crazy and killed a lot of people – sometimes Chet Huntley told about such things on the evening news – and of course there were Commies

The news industry of 1950s America has apparently made the fear of Communism and crime so common that even a little boy is aware of it. This is a significant starting point for a novel that explores so thoroughly the relationship between imagination and fear. It suggests that political anxiety is one of the clearest examples of how fear feeds on the human imagination.

In the course of Chapter 1, the author starts to dissect the workings of political fear, using the horror narrative as a scalpel. Only a few paragraphs after the passage quoted above, Georgie's fear of Commies and murderers is mentioned again, along with that other hate figure of mid-twentieth-century Americans, 'Japs'.

> So he walked down the four steps to the cellar shelf, his heart a warm, beating hammer in his throat, the hair on the nape of his neck standing at attention, his eyes hot, his hands cold, sure that at any moment the cellar door would swing shut on its own, closing off the white light falling through the kitchen windows, and then he would hear It, something worse than all the Commies and murderers in the world. Worse than Japs.

By mentioning Commies, murderers and Japs in the same sentence as a child's imaginary monster, does the author mean to suggest that these political fears may have an imaginary element too? It's not explicit, but the possibility is held out to us. Of course, we shouldn't forget that the monster in the cellar turns out to be real. Georgie is murdered by something very similar to the creature he imagined. Perhaps that means we should take political fears seriously too, rather than dismissing them as partially imagined or the product of a sensationalising news industry. Well, not entirely. As we saw in the previous chapter, 'It' is, in parts, a metaphor for the way stories take our fears and use them as to establish a hold over us. That is a perfect metaphysical expression of the way fears about Commies and murderers have established a hold over the society around Georgie.

Later in the novel, we see an example of how these same political hate figures expand and become more terrifying with every story told about them.

> An unsheathed Japanese sword lay across Butch's lap, a war souvenir which, Butch said, he had taken off the body of a dying Nip on the island of Tarawa (he had actually traded six bottles of Budweiser and three joysticks for the sword in Honolulu). Lately Butch almost always got out his sword when he drank. And since all of the boys, including Henry himself, were secretly convinced that sooner or later he would use it on someone, it was best to be far away when it made its appearance on Butch's lap.

Henry Bowers's father is a troubled man. He violently abuses his son. Perhaps his violent behaviour is linked to wartime experiences at the hands of the 'Japs', perhaps not. But what we do know is that his anecdotes about the war have been deliberately shaped to accentuate the fearsomeness of the enemy. In fact, his abusive actions are a constant retelling of that exaggerated story – he has become the embodiment of the terrifying qualities he ascribes to the Japanese. In that sense, he's rather like 'It' shaping itself to resemble an object of fear.

We saw in the first passage quoted above that the news industry is, in the author's estimation, involved in the propagation of political fears. Further on in Chapter 1, King takes a moment to pick apart the workings of that process, although the brief episode in question doesn't relate directly to politics, it concerns a journalist who's reporting on Georgie's death.

> ... there could have been no one down there, the County Sheriff would later exclaim to a Derry News reporter with a frustrated fury

so great it was almost agony; Hercules himself would have been swept away in that driving current ...

In this tiny vignette, the mechanism by which the news industry propagates fear is laid bare. In order to satisfy the journalist, the Sheriff feels compelled to engage in exaggeration and high-flown conceits about 'Hercules'. We're witnessing the birth of a news monster, and it's tempting to think that fears associated with 'Commies', murderers and 'Japs' are birthed in the same way.

I'll conclude this discussion of political fear by returning to the death of Georgie. It's interesting to note that the little boy's boat – the one that got him into so much trouble by floating down the drain – is made from newspaper. Is Stephen King hinting at the way the news industry leads us deeper and deeper into a state of fearfulness? Personally, I think so. Admittedly it's an extremely brief and undemonstrative use of metaphor, but that is the way the author so often works in *IT* – subtle images that hardly draw attention to themselves but collectively add up to a rich layer of meaning.

Connecting Themes

So far, I've described four thematic layers that complement and interact with the overt meaning of the events in *IT* – namely, the social layer, the psychological layer, the artistic layer and the political layer. As an endnote, I'd like to discuss two overarching themes that pull together all of those layers into one coherent whole. Most novelists consider that they have done a pretty good job if they manage to weave one unifying theme into their narrative. Typically, Stephen King's overflowing genius has provided us with two in *IT*.

The first of these unifying themes is the idea that horrors can often be found lurking below the surface of things. This kind of imagery is present from the very start of the novel – most memorably when Pennywise calls to Georgie from a drain. As the story proceeds, the main characters gradually discover that 'It' lives in the sewer under Derry. In fact, the tunnels are where the climactic action takes place, both in 1958 and 1985.

This physical imagery of subterranean evil arises totally naturally from the novel's main plot – the battle to rid a city and its inhabitants of a supernatural affliction – but it also perfectly expresses, in a metaphorical way, each of the layers of meaning in the novel. For example, the social layer of the novel expressed the idea that Derry has something fundamentally wrong with it – that it's the kind of place where people ignore or overlook terrible events going on all around them. The murder and vileness that people turn a blind eye to is, in a sense, below the surface of Derry society. It's also easy to see how the psychological layer connects with the image of subterranean evil. The traumas that the main characters experienced in childhood became buried in their unconscious minds, remaining below the level of normal thought and action but wreaking havoc with their lives in unexpected ways. The layer of the novel that explores artistic creation – specifically in horror fiction – is closely related to the psychological layer, as we have seen. The image of 'It' lurking in the filthy tunnels below the city and emerging from a toilet in the form of a werewolf is a perfect metaphor for the way horror movies and novels – like our dreams – produce terrifying echoes of our deepest fears.

The political layer of the novel is something of an orphan, failing to find its expression within the overarching theme of evil below the surface. Sometimes it's important not to overplay your hand as an author. The desire to illuminate too many aspects of the novel's meaning with a single metaphor can lead to a rather contrived feel.

The second unifying theme in *IT* is the idea of repetition – the notion that people's lives often go round and round in circles, with the same problematic behaviours appearing again and again. As we saw in our consideration of the psychological, social and artistic layers of the novel, one of the novel's central theses is that trauma can have a powerful hold on the consciousness. This is the engine that drives repeating patterns of behaviour for the novel's characters

The Losers are the most obvious cases of self-defeating repetition. In adulthood, all of them become stuck in loops of problematic behaviour. Bill feels guilt about the death of his brother and writes horror stories that re-enact the terrible things he experienced as a child; Bev seeks out abusive men like her father; Eddie seeks out clingy women like his mother; Ben is addicted to booze, having previously been addicted to comfort eating; Stan is oppressed by shame at his religion and Richie can't shake off the weird alter egos that haunt his imagination. At the heart of all their problems are the terrible events of their childhood – a sequence of horrific encounters with 'It'. As we've seen, this history of supernatural conflict mingles with their more ordinary psychological and social troubles from childhood (abuse, overprotective parents, obesity and so on). It is certainly a metaphor for those troubles, but also a possible cause of them and a possible consequence. The lack of clarity is deliberate and serves to inject great fascination and emotional charge into the theme of repetition.

Like the novel's main characters, the society that they come from, Derry, seems to go round in vicious circles. Mike reveals a pattern of mass murders indicating that 'It' wakes up and feeds every 27 years. As with the individual characters, the city's supernatural oppression has a complex and ambiguous relationship with more natural pathologies – society-wide behaviours such as neglect of children, cruelty towards the poor and attacks on homosexuals. Once again, the supernatural is certainly a metaphor for those behaviours, but also a possible cause and a possible consequence. The novel refuses to clarify.

In order to explore these circular patterns, Stephen King spreads the novel's action across two timeframes, nearly thirty years apart. The events of 1985 more or less repeat those of 1958. In both years, the group get together – at the dam building in 1958 and the Chinese meal in 1985 – and gradually come to understand the supernatural origin of their life struggles. Then, after various encounters with 'It', they attack the creature in its subterranean home in both years, apparently destroying it.

This repetition of an almost identical narrative in both 1958 and 1985 comes about because the supernatural foe, 'It', was not destroyed first time round – the Losers were less than thorough in their 1958 attack. But there's a further supernatural element to the repetition, and this resonates powerfully with the psychological and social themes. I'm referring to the weird amnesia that the Losers experience between 1958 and 1985. They seem to have completely forgotten their childhood friends and experiences. It certainly has a supernatural feel, but there is also a very familiar and human dimension to it. After all, people have a tendency to forget older (perhaps more authentic) versions of themselves and their social relationships as they grow up. So, it seems the supernatural evil is, yet again, operating as both a metaphor for psychological

76

phenomena, but also a potential cause and a potential consequence. It's the ambiguity of the amnesia that makes it so thematically resonant.

As a final note about the idea of unifying themes, I'd like to point out that an author is under no obligation to use their overarching theme as a rainbow leading to the redemption of the main characters. In other words, there's no reason why you have to resolve the conflicts that pulls together. *IT* offers only a faint hope that repetition of problem behaviours can be escaped. As the story proceeds, we see more and more signs that the Losers are successfully filling in the gaps of their forgetfulness, overcoming their personal difficulties and resisting 'It'. They come together as a group, listen to one another's stories of struggle, and stick together in the face of mortal danger. But the fact that these healing experiences take place twice in the course of the novel, almost identically, and are followed by another descent into amnesia, makes one suspect that there would be more repetitions ahead in a hypothetical future after the end of the novel.

Takeaway

- Ideas that connect the world of the novel with the real world enrich the reading experience of a horror novel – there can be multiple layers of thematic meaning.
  - Social themes
    - Blur the distinction between human evil and supernatural evil.
    - Provide characters who contrast with evil.
  - Psychological themes
    - Shape each manifestation of supernatural evil so that it functions as a powerful metaphor for psychological suffering.
    - Also provide metaphors for sources of psychological healing.
  - Artistic themes
    - Consider making the hero a writer.
    - Make the 'big evil' a metaphor for horror fiction.
    - Reference other stories that have the same underlying themes as yours – directly and in

details.

- Allow some characters to comment on the nature of horror almost like critics.

o Political themes
  - Hint at the horror elements of the story when mentioning politics.
  - Hint at political matters in the details of the horror elements.

o Connecting themes
  - In a variety of different contexts, repeatedly use imagery that hints at a key feature of the 'big evil'.

3. CHARACTER

'... they stand there for awhile longer, feeling the power that is in their
circle, the closed body that they make.'
– Stephen King, *IT*

Great characters are the foundation all popular literature. There are
two reasons for that. Firstly, character is the raw material from
which an author has to spin a thread of plot. You can't create a
convincing story without a rich character that presents all sorts of
possibilities for struggle. Secondly, fascination with character is
what keeps people reading to the last page. When we're locked
onto a character, we naturally want to follow them right to the end
of their travels, even if we've already worked out where that
journey is likely to end. For these two reasons, it's important to
accomplish two goals in your novel. Firstly, make sure that the
hero is a stand-out presence. You should put the majority of your
effort into creating rich and distinctive main character. Secondly,
make it easy for readers to connect emotionally with your
characters. This chapter will look at the techniques used in *IT* to
achieve those goals.

Why a Group?
Stephen King sets himself a somewhat unusual challenge in *IT*. He
has a group of seven characters, all of whom can be classified as
protagonists (heroes/heroines). Having only one character in the
limelight is difficult enough, as we all know; defining their motives

and guiding them through a logical sequence of actions is like a puzzle. Doing the same with two characters is exponentially more difficult. But juggling the demands of seven characters is a technical tour de force, and we can learn a lot from studying how Stephen King does it.

The first and most obvious question to ask is, why would you inflict such a writing challenge on yourself? The simple answer is that, in *IT*, the idea of a group coming together and overcoming evil is part of the meaning of the novel – a theme with relevance for at least two of the layers discussed in the last chapter.

There are no fewer than two major plot turning points that focus in on the significance of the group. That should tell you something about its importance as a theme. The first is the building of the dam in chapters 7 and 8. During this episode, the kids overcome the social isolation forced on them by bullies, and open up to one another about their supernatural experiences and psychological torments. It's left to Richie Tozier to pin down the significance of this plot moment. Looking back as an adult in Chapter 8, section 2, he remembers how Mr Nell, the police officer, showed up at the Barrens. The kid version of Richie decided to take the blame for flooding the town – with fateful consequences.

> When, Richie wonders, did it become too late to turn back? When he and Stan showed up and pitched in, helping to build the dam? When Bill told them how the school picture of his brother had turned its head and winked? Maybe ... but to Rich Tozier it seems that the dominoes really began to fall when Ben Hanscom stepped forward and said 'I showed them ... how to do it. It's my fault.'

This noble gesture encourages the others to come together in solidarity. Every one of the kids steps up and claims equal responsibility for the damage caused by the (imaginary) flood. As Richie the adult correctly points out, this gelling of the group is the moment that sets in motion all the events of the latter part of the novel. It really does feel like dominoes falling, to use his phrase. Having shared their supernatural experiences, they're encouraged to push the solidarity even further. Bill and Richie together visit Georgie's room to look at the photo album. They also go to Neibolt Street to see if they can track down the 'leper' who scared Eddie. After those experiences, the novel moves inevitably towards the two showdowns between 'It' and the group.

The second plot moment that emphasises the importance of the group is the reunion in Chapter 10. The fact that this occurs at the midpoint – one of the most resonant parts of many popular novels and movies – is a confirmation of the theme's significance. In many ways, the meal in the Chinese restaurant is a rerun of the dam building. The adult Losers once again gel as a group by sharing personal information about their struggles. The result is an acceleration towards conflict with 'It' – as we can tell from the ghastly apparitions that crawl out of their fortune cookies at the end of the meal.

Juggling multiple main characters is such an unusual and difficult literary challenge that there really has to be a thematic justification of the kind we've just seen. And, to avoid leaving the reader with a sense of incoherence, the thematic significance of the group needs to be signalled loud and clear, preferably at prominent turning points in the story.

Group Dynamics

You'll know from your own experience, as a reader of novels and a viewer of movies, that heroes need to undergo significant development in the course of a story if they're going to remain interesting and leave the reader with a sense of having made a worthwhile journey. It's a complicated process, but one that must be mastered, as it's more important to the success of a story than just about anything else. Tensions within the character drive changes, and those changes give rise to further tension, and so on. You could call it the engine of story. In a way, a group of protagonists functions very much like a character. The group experiences tensions that lead to change, and that change leads to further tension, which drives story.

For a single protagonist, tension can take one of two main forms. Internal conflict and external conflict. But internal conflict also breaks down into two varieties. Firstly, it can be a conflict between different 'levels' of the character's life – for example, between their psychological motivations and their practical circumstances. Think of Luke Skywalker in the 1979 movie *Star Wars*, who yearns for adventure, but knows that his aunt and uncle depend on him for help around the farm. Secondly, the source of internal tension could be a conflict between contradictory influences within the same level of the character's life – for example, between different psychological drives. Think of Indiana Jones, who craves professional success as an archaeologist but fears snakes.

With a group of protagonists, tensions are created in a very similar way. The group can experience internal conflict and conflict with external forces. But internal conflicts, once again, take two different forms. Firstly, there can be conflicts between different aspects of the group's life – for example, between personal animosity and a professional task. Secondly, a group can experience a tug of war over one particular aspect of its life – for example, an agreement over how to approach a professional task. But, in all of these cases, the result is a behaviour change within the group, which leads to further tension.

In *IT*, most of the tension comes in the form of conflict with forces from outside the group. It takes the form of negative social, psychological and supernatural influences on the individual members of the group – and to some extent on the group as a whole. The effect of these external tensions is to compress the group, changing its behaviour so that it becomes more unified. In section 8 of Chapter 7, we see an important admission by several of the kids that they've had similar encounters with the clown. They draw closer by sharing stories that have been guilty secrets up to that point. Similarly, in section 3 of Chapter 8, there's a kind of therapy taking place within the group as Richie attempts to make Bill feel better about the death of his brother. Importantly, the consolidation of the group sets off a process of changing behaviour and increased tension with external forces. In section 6 of Chapter 16, we see the group as a whole coming under attack from Eddie's mother.

> 'They're bad friends, Eddie!' she cried in a near-frenzy. 'I know that, I feel that with all my heart, they'll bring you nothing but pain and grief!'

But that is just a prelude to more terrifying attacks on the group as a whole, which are mounted by 'It'. The creature makes clear in Chapter 21, section 1, that it was hurt and enraged by the attack on Neibolt Street. It promises a savage reprisal against the whole group when they arrive in the tunnels.

When they got here It would cast them, shrieking and insane, into the deadlights.

It tries hard in both 1958 and 1985 to bring that about, but without success. However, its aggressive onslaught does bring about a change in the group's behaviour. They display a new level of intimacy by engaging in a shared sexual experience. It's a scene that has become highly controversial for many readers and critics, and it certainly seems like something written in a former age, but one can appreciate that it fits into the structure of the story and the role of the group within it. The Losers become closer and closer by encountering and overcoming mounting threats, until the ultimate threat is defeated and the group, correspondingly, achieves an ultimate form of unity.

In addition to tensions with the outside world, the group experiences a degree of internal conflict. Richie's hardball banter is the main focus of it. For the reader, his obnoxious language represents a worrying identity crisis for the group – a failure to agree on the rules of decent behaviour. And it's not just a trivial matter of name-calling either. It is, after all, not that different from some of the things Henry Bowers and the other bullies say. Richie's knockabout teasing is even repeated by 'It' to get a reaction from Ben and, later, Mike. This example is from Chapter 11, section 1.

> The clown shrieked laughter again. 'Kill me? Kill me?' And suddenly, horribly, the voice was Richie Tozier's voice, not his voice, precisely, but Richie Tozier doing his Pickaninny Voice: 'Doan kill me, massa, I be a good nigguh, doan kill thisyere black boy, Haystack!' Then that shrieking laughter again.

The change in behaviour that these internal tensions provoke is low key. The phrase 'beep beep' is the group's shorthand way of telling Richie that he's gone too far. This illustrates another point about group interaction – that it must, sometimes, have a low emotional temperature if it's going to convince and compel the audience. Constant psychodrama would undermine believability and empathy. However, a really skilful author will ensure that the group dynamics faintly echo the bigger tensions of the novel even at those lighter, more playful moments.

Another way of ensuring that group tensions keep our interest without exhausting our emotions is to bury them a little below the surface of events. In *IT*, there is a subtle undertone of sexual jealousy between the boys over Bev. It's never openly discussed between them, but it is communicated in other ways. In the aftermath of the attack on 'It' at Neibolt Street in Chapter 18, section 10, Bev asks for a shirt to cover herself up.

> 'Sh-sh-sure,' Bill said. He pulled his white t-shirt over his head,
> …
> 'Thank you, Bill,' she said, and for one hot, smoking moment their eyes locked directly. Bill did not look away this time. His gaze was firm, adult.
> 'W-W-W-Welcome,' he said.
> Good luck, Big Bill, Ben thought, and he turned away from that gaze. It was hurting him, hurting him in a deeper place than any Vampire or Werewolf would ever be able to reach. But all the same, there was such a thing as propriety. The word he didn't know; on the concept he was very clear. Looking at them when they were looking at each other that way would be as wrong as looking at her breasts when she let go of the front of her blouse to pull Bill's t-shirt over her head. If that's the way it is. But you'll never love her the way I do. Never.

Ben's act of turning away as he sees Bill's almost-adult connection with Bev is a tiny gesture, but it speaks volumes about the emotions seething beneath the surface of the group. Understatement of this kind is usually best when evoking tensions – especially if your aim is to provide a quiet parallel to bigger battles and stronger tensions.

Individual Stories

Although, in many ways, the group of protagonists created by Stephen King seems to behave like a single entity, defined by its group dynamics and group interactions with outside forces, we also get a clear sense of each character as an individual with a separate story.

The strongest of these stories is definitely Bill's. This reflects the fact that there's a clear hierarchy within the group. It's a truth that's acknowledged by other group members. This is Richie's thought on the subject from Chapter 7, section 8.

> Bill was their leader, the guy they all looked up to. No one said so

out loud; no one needed to. But Bill was the idea man, the guy who could think of something to do on a boring day, the guy who remembered games the others had forgotten.

So, it's not surprising that Bill's story has a prominence beyond that of the others' stories. In fact, it is so important that it has a unique role within the structure of the novel.

As early as section 2 of Chapter 1, we're given an insight into the strong emotional connection that Bill has with his brother Georgie.

> 'Juh juh-Georgie?'
> George turned back to look at his brother.
> 'Be c-careful.'
> 'Sure.' His brow creased a little. That was something your mom said, not your big brother. It was as strange as him giving Bill a kiss.
> 'Sure I will.'
> He went out. Bill never saw him again.

And at the opposite end of the novel, in Chapter 21, section 9, there's a corresponding moment that connects right back to this momentary display of closeness.

> It was George wavering up the tunnel toward him, George, still dressed in his blood-spattered yellow rainslicker. One sleeve dangled limp and useless. George's face was white as cheese and his eyes were shiny silver. They fixed on Bill's own.
> 'My boat!' Georgie's lost voice rose, wavering, in the tunnel. 'I can't find it, Bill, I've looked everywhere and I can't find it and now I'm dead and it's your fault your fault YOUR FAULT –'
> 'Juh-Juh-Georgie!' Bill shrieked. He felt his mind tottering, ripping free of its moorings.

The emotional connection between those two moments is not only the spine of Bill's story but also the spine of the novel as a whole. Looking across the full span of the novel, we see various other episodes that support and re-energise that spine – for example, the investigation of Georgie's photo album, or Bill's attempt to kill 'It' at Neibolt Street. In the latter of those two episodes, Bill's anger over his kid brother's death is powerfully expressed.

> The gun went off again with a second deafening bang. Bill

Denbrough shouted, 'YOU KILLED MY BROTHER, YOU FUCKER!'

Bill may have primacy but he's only first among equals. The author doesn't neglect any of the other members of the Losers' Club. He spins a thread of personal narrative for each of them with just a few scenes. And every one of those scenes conveys an emotional charge that's personal to the character. For example, the spine of Bev's story is her experience of coming to sexual maturity; key scenes include the recollection of a sexually charged punishment from her father and the occasion when she stumbles upon a male masturbation game. Ben's story centres on his shame and self-isolation as an overweight child; its key moments are a trip to the library and a beating by the school bully. Eddie is a psychosomatic asthmatic; we see his anger at the pharmacist for handing out a placebo treatment, and, later, we witness his rejection of an over-protective mother. Mike's story illustrates how one can remain a human being while surrounded by evil; we're given a loving account of his family's yearly work on the land, and many episodes reveal his sense of public duty. Richie has a poor relationship with his emotionally distant father; in one family scene, we hear how he acts the clown just to get some attention. Stanley is a Jewish boy who routinely gets teased for his religion; a neat and organised approach to life helps him cope – particularly his birdwatching hobby – although, ultimately, he commits suicide.

As these personal stories extend through the novel, they occasionally give rise to scenes that feature two or three of the kids. Depending on the circumstances, the focus may remain on one particular kid, or the scene could feature elements of more than one character's story. In the scene where Bill explores Georgie's photo album, he's accompanied by Richie. Here, the focus is on Bill's guilt feelings about the death of his brother. Later, during the first encounter with 'It' at Neibolt Street, Bill and Richie are together again, and, this time, the scene draws in aspects of both boys' stories – Richie's experience of 'It' is influenced by his recent trip to see a werewolf movie, whereas Bill's is influenced by the clown seen in his brother's photo album. Ben and Bev are also involved in several small-group scenes together. Ben's shy admiration of Bev is a feature of his personal story, and it naturally draws them together. For example, there's a short scene in which he can barely bring himself to talk to her at the end of the school year. Ben's infatuation is everything in this scene, excluding Bev's personal story altogether. Later, the stories of Ben, Bev and Richie coincide for their visit to the movie theatre. All their stories contribute a little something to the emotional landscape in this case – Richie's need to get money from his sardonic father, Bev's awareness of her sexual attractiveness as she teases Richie for asking her out and Ben's awkwardness around Bev. Later still, it is Ben, Bev and Eddie who come together, playing at pitching pennies until Bev is insulted by another kid – another scene dominated by Ben's romantic feelings as he springs to her defence.

The effect of these ensemble scenes is, firstly, to provide variety, and, secondly, to bridge the gap between the individual character stories and the story of the group. For these two reasons, they make a major contribution to the success of the 'group of protagonists' in *IT*. Ultimately, the novel is about the group, and it is only the group's story that rises to a climax of action. The individual stories of the kids feed into and become consumed in that climax.

Speech

It's a strange fact that, regardless of whether a character is good or evil, attractive or repellent, readers are happy to connect with them emotionally and follow them to the end of the novel if they're drawn in a convincing and individualised way. In my opinion, speech patterns have a very important role to play in this. I've identified a number of related techniques in *IT*.

As you might expect, a core technique for creating convincing and individualised character through speech is to listen carefully to the sounds made by speakers in the real world and find a way of recreating them on the page using non-standard spellings and other special effects. In *IT*, the rendering of Bill's stutter is a great example. It's so beautifully done that I can only think Stephen King must have done some keen observation before including it in the novel.

> 'E-E-Eddie's muh-hum is w-w-worried that h-he's g-gonna break and sh-she wuh-hon't be able to g-get a re-re-refund.'

When it comes to finding written equivalents for the sounds that you hear in a real-world way of speaking, it's generally more effective to select just one or two key mannerisms and use them sparingly. By contrast, Stephen King has thrown all caution to the winds for the rendering of Bill's voice. On the page his words hold up your eye, demanding that you sound them out to yourself. He's unique in having such a convincing and individualised sound identity. The novel does render certain other characters' accents through non-standard spelling, but it's done in an extremely fragmentary way – nothing like the uncompromising representation of Bill's stutter – and they tend to be individuals with 'walk on parts' in the story. For most characters in *IT*, we have absolutely no idea what their voices sound like. The fact that Bill has been given this strong sound identity makes it clear that he has a special status. He is, as we've seen, the de facto leader of the Losers, and his personal story is identical with the spine of the novel.

But the stutter is about more than just signalling Bill's importance. I believe it has a significance in its own right. When I first read the novel, I viewed it as a symptom of Bill's guilt and anger – a problem that gets resolved when Georgie's death is avenged. But then it occurred to me that Bill was even stuttering before Georgie's death. So, perhaps it's a kind of emblem of the novel's theme of repetition – words getting stuck just like the human beings in the novel. If you accept my interpretation, then the convincing and individualised depiction of Bill – largely a product of his speech patterns – is more than just a tactic for gripping the reader; it's a means of giving the character a deeper thematic resonance.

But creating a convincing and individualised character is not just about using non-standard spellings and other special effects. It's probably more important to focus on the words and phrases that the character uses. By selecting vocabulary and expressions that are instantly recognisable and radiate personality, you can go a long way to creating a character that readers will form an emotional bond with. To explore that idea further, let's consider the Losers' Club in their childhood phase. Here's a couple of examples of their typical style of speech, which are taken from the dam-building sequence in Chapter 7, section 2. Bill is trying to rouse his fellow dam builders after a lunch break.

'… are you g-g-gonna si-hit there on your b-big c-c-can all d-day?'

...

> 'Okay,' he said. 'You guys want to take your shoes off, because you're gonna get your little footsies wet.'

It's a good-natured but caustic way of speaking that's instantly recognisable. It also uses vocabulary that's saturated with the identity of the speaker. For example, Bill uses the word 'can' in preference to 'ass' or some similar term. The word is perfectly judged. It's a little on the indelicate side but it couldn't be described as vulgar. In fact, it's precisely the sort of thing that boisterous schoolboys from a good background would have said in a more innocent age.

In addition to their memorable and characterful quality, those utterances just quoted have a couple of features that enhance a reader's willingness to connect emotionally with Bill. Firstly, the tone is funny – a quality that is always welcome in friends. A funny character will almost always carry readers with them. Secondly, the smart-mouth way of speaking will be familiar to many people from their own childhoods. It's impossible not to feel a little nostalgia, and occasionally laugh out loud, as you listen to the young Losers slapping one another down. That's a great basis for friendship.

As mentioned earlier, distinctive and individualising speech is just as effective for unlikeable characters. It encourages readers to form an emotional connection of a different kind, but the relationship is just as strong and enduring. Henry Bowers is a perfect example. He hooks readers in through a sort of characterful viciousness.

> 'Go ahead, yell,' Henry said. 'You'll be pickin your fuckin guts off your sneakers.'

The two-dimensional vulgarities suggest low IQ, while the blending of extreme violence ('guts') and kid-centric details ('sneakers') evokes juvenile sadism. It's an obnoxious but highly individual way of speaking that makes us want to stick around and see Henry get his comeuppance.

It's also important to note that even characters who are fantastical and therefore utterly unfamiliar can use a tone and vocabulary that individualises them and helps readers bond. This is important in a horror novel, where some of the speaking characters are more than likely going to be otherworldly. For example, what

could be more individual than the Turtle's phlegmatic tone and
new-agey vocabulary?

What are you?
– I'm the Turtle, son. I made the universe, but please don't blame
me for it; I had a bellyache.
Help me! Please help me!
– I take no stand in these matters.
My brother –
– has his own place in the macroverse; energy is eternal, as even a
child such as yourself must understand

Viewpoint

In 19th-century novels, it was usual to find narration that seemed to
be coming from some god-like, all-knowing, all-seeing source.
Open any work by Dickens, Hardy, Trollope or Scott and you'll see
what I mean. The voice hovers over the world of the novel, often
providing moral direction to the reader. It was a style of storytelling
that expressed the spirit of a more hierarchical age. But, these days,
readers are reluctant to accept that kind of heavy authority. For
comparison, open up any piece of contemporary genre fiction,
select a scene at random and think about the quality of the
narrative voice. The chances are, you'll find that a distinctive
personality comes through the words on the page. And, usually,
that personality will be closely associated with one of the characters
in the scene. I don't mean the narrator is always identical with one
of the characters, I mean that the narrative voice seems to be
shadowing the thoughts of a particular character and looking
through their eyes. That will be true even if the narration is
delivered in the third person (he, she, it). As events are related, the
character's personality traits will be subtly colouring the
description. This approach to narration has one big benefit that's
not easy to achieve with authoritative 19th-century-style narration.
It encourages readers to connect emotionally with key characters in
the novel – even characters who are unlikeable. When readers
develop feelings of empathy for key characters, they're more likely
to follow their story right to the end.

Without a doubt, Stephen King is a master of the art of
immersing readers in a viewpoint character's consciousness. In the
work of less experienced authors, you often run into passages
where you realise the narration has drifted and is no longer

channelling a character's personality – the illusion has broken down and what the reader experiences is an intrusion of the author's own consciousness. But in *IT*, the effect is seamless. So, what techniques does Stephen King deploy to create this beguiling illusion of being in a character's head?

In fact, the toolkit for creating immersive, characterful narration is very similar to that associated with speech. That makes sense, given that good narration is essentially the voice, or internal monologue, of a particular character. So, for example, the use of vocabulary that seems natural for a particular viewpoint character will help evoke their personality – even in a third-person description. The following example is from a section in which a barman has the viewpoint.

> Mr Hanscom took hold of the stein and drained it. He should have been flat on his keister

In just this brief quotation, there are two examples of characterful vocabulary. The formal description 'Mr Hanscom' immediately positions us very close to the barman's consciousness. Then, in the next sentence, we see the highly characteristic word 'keister'. It has a hard-bitten quality that's unmistakably blue collar – perfect for a barman.

Another technique associated with immersive, characterful narration is to focus only on things that are of interest to the viewpoint character. Moreover, any attitudes or judgements implied by the description should be fully in keeping with the viewpoint character's likely attitudes. Again, this is not so very different from the speech technique of remaining faithful to a character's tone of voice. The start of Chapter 21 provides a perfect example. We are immersed in the thoughts of 'It'.

> Something new had happened.
> For the first time in forever, something new.
> Before the universe there had been only two things. One was Itself and the other was the Turtle. The Turtle was a stupid old thing that never came out of its shell. It thought that maybe the Turtle was dead, had been dead for the last billion years or so. Even if it wasn't, it was still a stupid old thing, and even if the Turtle had vomited the universe out whole, that didn't change the fact of its stupidity.

We have no idea who, what or where 'It' is, and the author refuses to fill us in. Why should he provide that sort of information? At this point, his narration is supposed to be reflecting the consciousness of 'It', and there's no way 'It' would be dwelling on those subjects. What does concern it is the threat from the kids, and that is what the narration focuses on. Moreover, it is very clear what 'It' thinks about the kids and their potential ally the Turtle. The repetition of 'something new' reveals a certain spluttering fascination with the audacious attackers. And the repetition of 'stupid' three times suggests a sort of childish petulance. It's a vivid and economical portrait of the viewpoint character, achieved exclusively through the tone and vocabulary of the narration. This is a fantastic example of how even truly unlikeable characters can become compelling if you let the reader into their head.

Not all narration in *IT* sticks as close to the viewpoint character's consciousness as the examples given above. Some passages have deliberately been written in such a way that the narration stands off a little from the viewpoint character. Perhaps unexpectedly, this is a style that Stephen King frequently uses to follow a character's internal monologue. It's big on phrases like 'he thought'. Using words like that draws attention to the viewpoint character as a separate entity rather than immersing us in their consciousness. As a result, we're distanced from the ideas being described and find ourselves less inclined to empathise with them. For example, in section 1 of Chapter 3, Stan receives his call about the return of 'It' from Mike. We see the call from his wife's perspective.

> As his smile faded she recognized – or thought she did – his analytic expression, the one which said someone was unfolding a problem or explaining a sudden change in an ongoing situation or telling him something strange and interesting. This last was probably the case, she gathered. A new client? An old friend? Perhaps. She turned her attention back to the TV, where a woman was flinging her arms around Richard Dawson and kissing him madly. She thought that Richard Dawson must get kissed even more than the Blarney stone. She also thought she wouldn't mind kissing him herself.

Although Stan's wife is not demonised in any way, it feels as though we're meant to maintain a certain emotional distance from her response to the telephone call. Imagine the same episode described without phrases like 'she recognized', 'she gathered' and 'she thought'. The opening might be expressed as follows: 'Something like that old, familiar analytic expression crossed his face.' We would certainly be more inclined to feel empathy for her loving concern and eventual realisation that she had misinterpreted Stan's state of mind. But that's not what the author wants. His decision to use a slightly distancing mode of narration for this viewpoint character at this moment is significant. All the marriage partners mentioned in the novel – Bill's, Eddie's, Bev's and Stan's – fail to understand the importance of the Losers' Club and their promise. They are outsiders and they know it. It evokes strong reactions in all of them. The exclusion of the partners from the group serves to reinforce our impression of the group's unity. It is, therefore, entirely appropriate that the style of narration at this moment in the novel should effectively warn us not to empathise too much with Stan's wife. She is, as the action of the scene confirms, an outsider in relation to the struggle against 'It'.

Among experts on creative writing, one of the most common pieces of advice is that you should not swap in and out of different viewpoint characters within the same scene. There is a certain truth in this. It can be a sign that the author has allowed the seamless illusion of being in a character's head to break down. However, there are certain instances where 'head hopping', as it is often called, can be a desirable special effect.

The opening pages of *IT* are one such occasion. The novel begins with a very curious sentence.

> The terror, which would not end for another twenty-eight years – if it ever did end – began, so far as I know or can tell, with a boat made from a sheet of newspaper floating down a gutter swollen with rain.

Who is the speaker? It's clearly not a 19th-century-style all-knowing, all-seeing narrator, because it seems to be someone who is involved in the world of the novel – it uses the first-person pronoun (I) and appears uncertain about facts. And yet, the speaker is clearly outside the events being described, in the sense that they're able to look back over a long span of time that covers the whole novel and beyond. The mystery of their identity is never resolved. Perhaps, having read the whole novel, one could argue that it is Mike, but we don't read novels backwards, so, to the fresh reader, this voice remains a mysterious, somewhat detached presence.

No sooner has this speaker been evoked than a new narrative viewpoint is adopted. It's that of Georgie.

> The rain had not stopped, but it was finally slackening. It tapped on the yellow hood of the boy's slicker, sounding to his ears like rain on a shed roof ... a comfortable, almost cozy sound.

We're literally inside the boy's hood with him. But a couple of paragraphs later, it's back to the original speaker. It develops into something of a journalistic voice, commenting on the reaction of neighbours and public officials to the flooding.

> ... many people in Derry had begun to make nervous jokes about arks. The Public Works Department had managed to keep Jackson Street open, but Witcham was impassable from the sawhorses all the way to the center of town.

Then, an extraordinary thing happens.

> George had to sprint to keep up with it. Water sprayed out from beneath his galoshes in muddy sheets. Their buckles made a jolly jingling as George Denbrough ran toward his strange death.

We've clearly returned to Georgie's viewpoint, but, suddenly and shockingly, the more knowing narrator breaks through with a macabre message about George Denbrough running towards his death. It's so brutal that it's almost as though the journalistic voice is committing an act of violence on young Georgie.

In my view, this expressive use of multiple viewpoints is a masterpiece of craft. It breaks one of the cardinal 'rules' of good writing – the idea that you should stick with one viewpoint for a whole scene – but it does so in order to dramatise the content of that scene. The author begins by evoking a mysterious, unidentified watcher. He then puts us in the head of a little boy at play. Then the watcher appears again, almost as though they are stalking the child, and wields the threat of a horrible death.

This is not the only instance of expressive head hopping in *IT*.

Generally, the author uses the technique to create an impression that the Losers' Club are a close-knit group, thinking and acting in close coordination – for example, during the dam building. Consider the following example. One page into the section describing the kids' lunch break by the Kenduskeag, we're in a space that encompasses the thoughts of both Eddie and Bill.

> Both Eddie and Bill had been amazed by the size of the repast Ben had laid out with businesslike efficiency

But a couple of paragraphs further on, we're in Ben's head.

> The thought of wasting his money on such a nonessential item cast momentary gloom across Ben's face.

These aren't really changes of viewpoint. They're changes of emphasis in the narration of a group consciousness.

There is also a fascinating sequence describing events around the murder of Adrian Mellon at the Canal Days festival in Chapter 2. But this is not so much head hopping as a series of very short scenes, with each successive one given to a new viewpoint. As we will see in a later chapter, short scenes are used to great effect by Stephen King as a means of expressing theme and emotion.

Infected by Evil

Having encouraged you to do everything possible to establish a strong connection between readers and a novel's main characters, I'm now going tell you to consider doing the exact opposite. Giving an otherwise likeable protagonist a side to their character that's barely distinguishable from the novel's 'big evil' can be uncomfortable for readers. Nevertheless, it's a useful strategy. It can complicate the moral landscape in fascinating and compelling ways. For one thing, nobody likes a Peter Perfect. If readers are honest, they're probably more convinced by a protagonist or group of protagonists with an imperfection or weak link. Also, this strategy of infecting heroes with a little evil can create a sense of moral jeopardy, suggesting that even the good guys might fall into bad ways – the more risk and drama the better.

In *IT*, Richie's character is used in exactly this way. If we see the group of friends as a combined hero, Richie is the weak link that stops them becoming insufferably victimy and self-righteous. His behaviour also implies that it might not take much for one of the Losers to become one of the disciples of Henry Bowers. The lure of the dark side is always a fascinating plot device.

In both childhood and adulthood scenes, it's clear that the other Losers find his behaviour rather disturbing on occasions. In Chapter 8, section 10, we first hear them using the phrase 'beep beep'. It's their warning to Richie that his behaviour has become just a little too anarchic. It derives, of course, from the *Roadrunner* cartoon, famous for its crazy, destructive action. I admit it's hardly a damning indictment to be compared to a cartoon. But remember that we've already seen another of the novel's characters being described in a similar way, namely Pennywise himself. Georgie noticed, in Chapter 1, that the clown was wearing gloves like Mickey Mouse or Donald Duck.

This rather subtle parallel between Richie and Pennywise is just the beginning. As a reader, it's sometimes difficult to share the tolerance of Richie displayed by the other Losers. He frequently displays a silly-sinister quality that's reminiscent of Pennywise the clown. For example, he has a host of imaginary characters that he slips into from time to time – a behaviour that faintly echoes the way 'It' shifts between manifestations. Moreover, those imaginary characters – 'Kinky Briefcase' and the others – have a disturbing quality that's unsettling in the same way that a scary clown is unsettling. The voices and mannerisms that Richie puts on remind one of the lisping silliness of Pennywise. In one particularly chilling example, the word 'Kee-rash' is used to describe a breaking window from Richie's point of view (Chapter 8, section 7). This is strikingly similar to the word 'Kee-rect' used by Pennywise (Chapter 1, section 3).

But the parallel between Richie and Pennywise becomes even more explicit than that. In Chapter 11, section 4, he reflects that, even as a grown man, he feels compelled to slip into a clown role that he played as a child.

> The others saw him as the Klass Klown, the Krazy Kut-up, and he had fallen neatly and easily into that role again.

It's disturbing enough that he links himself to the idea of clownishness, but, later in the same section, he uses some highly revealing imagery to talk about his own thought processes. He speaks as though his mind contained a mini Pennywise whose manic behaviour needs to be restrained and redirected.

> ... he had begun to understand the great principle that moved the universe, at least that part of the universe which had to do with careers and success: you found the crazy guy who was running around inside of you, fucking up your life. You chased him into a corner and grabbed him. But you didn't kill him. Oh no. Killing was too good for the likes of that little bastard. You put a harness over his head and then started plowing. The crazy guy worked like a demon once you had him in the traces.

Is this talk of a 'crazy guy' and a 'demon' purely metaphorical, or something more? Something supernatural? Chilling potential explanations for Richie's clownishness start to come to mind.

But apart from a certain clownishness, does Richie engage in any particularly problematic behaviour that might justify aligning him with 'It' in the reader's mind? The simple answer is yes, he does. On quite a few occasions, he brings a distinctly unpleasant tone to the interactions of the group. Even allowing for the fact that, as we all know, there's often an amoral element to childhood behaviour, and further allowing for the fact that these events are supposed to have taken place in the 1950s, a period with rather different social attitudes, there's a disturbing quality to Richie's words from time to time.

> 'This here's Stan the Man Uris,' Richie told Ben. 'Stan's a Jew. Also, he killed Christ.'

This kind of obnoxious talk may be laughed off by the others as a joke or an attempt to shock, but it's uncomfortably reminiscent of the bullying meted out by the likes of Henry Bowers – the thug who later becomes enslaved to 'It'. I wouldn't have been at all surprised if Stephen King had chosen to write a scene in which 'It' points out to Richie that he and Henry are 'not so very different'. Perhaps that's just as well, since scenes of that kind have become something of a cliché. Nevertheless, we're provided with a host of opportunities to draw that same conclusion for ourselves. Here's a particularly nasty example.

Salaaming frantically in front of the startled and embarrassed Ben Hanscom, Richie was speaking in what he called his Nigger Jim Voice.

'Lawks-a-mussy, it's be Haystack Calhoun!' Richie screamed. 'Don't fall on me, Mistuh Haystack, suh! You'se gwineter cream me if you do! Lawks-a-mussy, lawks-a-mussy! Three hunnert pounds of swaingin meat, eighty-eight inches from tit to tit, Haystack be smellin jest like a loader panther shit! I'se gwineter leadjer inter de raing, Mistuh Haystack, suh! I'se sho enuf gwineter leadjer! Jest don'tchoo be fallin on dis yere black boy!'

Compare that with some words uttered by 'It' to Mike.

'Hello dere, howyadoon?' Pennywise screamed from the dangling, swinging phone. 'Howyadoon, you dirty coon? Hello

They really are 'not so very different'.

Over the course of the novel. we see Richie swaying back and forth between good and evil. His obnoxiousness is tolerated by the other Losers – and by the reader – because it's mixed in with more positive behaviour. But he could literally go either way. Towards the end of the novel, in Chapter 22, good enjoys a victory over evil within Richie's personality as he selflessly drags Bill back from the edge of the deadlights. But it's only temporary. When he talks with Mike by phone in the Last Interlude, you suspect that me might break out into offensive remarks about Jews at any moment.

'What was Stan's last name?' I asked him.

…

Then Richie said, uncertainly: 'I think it was Underwood, but that isn't Jewish, is it?'

'It was Uris.'

As promised, Stephen King has greatly complicated the moral landscape of his novel. He offers us only an uncertain hope for human goodness. If the Losers no longer possess the qualities of selflessness and loyalty that allowed them to defeat the supernatural evil of 'It', could 'It' somehow make a comeback after another 27 years? This is a suitably chilling backdrop to the horror narrative.

Takeaway

- Great characters allow you to spin out a thread of narrative and hook readers.
  - Why a group?
    - Only consider using a group of main characters if the story provides a sound reason for doing so.
  - Group dynamics
    - Create conflicts between the various levels of your main character's / group's internal life.
    - Create conflicts between contending influences on one level of the main character's / group's internal life.
    - Create sources of external conflict for the main character / group.
  - Individual stories
    - A group of main characters requires a 'first among equals', but give all of them a well-defined story.
    - Create ensemble scenes for different combinations of group members.
  - Speech
    - Speech is one of the best ways to create convincing and individualised characters.
      - Observe real speech sounds but reserve this technique for important characters.
      - Use characteristic tone and vocabulary.
      - Don't neglect the speech of villains and fantastical characters – make it individual too.
  - Viewpoint
    - Saturate the narration with the personality of the viewpoint character.
    - Make the narration stand off from a character's viewpoint if we are meant to feel alienated from them.
    - Feel free to use head-hopping in group-

focused scenes.

- o Infected by evil
  - Parallels between the 'big evil' and a main character can complicate the moral landscape interestingly.

4. PLACE AND TIME

'Adrian might think Derry was a great place, but it scared Don.'
— Stephen King, *IT*

Detailed, naturalistic description of setting is the general rule throughout most of *IT*, but there's a marked emphasis on social rather than physical setting. Physical description is only a priority for certain types of story moment, and for the description of certain key locations – specifically, locations that draw on the horror genre's rich literary and cinematic traditions.

Social Setting
For Stephen King, naturalism is about building up a large number of details that combine to become a convincing collage. The piling up of details in *IT* can be so intense that it sometimes seems to be an end in itself. You sense an insatiable curiosity about the world, and a definite affection for certain times and places. However, his greatest passion is clearly for social environment rather than physical setting. By 'social environment' I mean behaviours and attitudes. This type of information is just as much part of our sense of setting as physical information. That's true in both life and fiction. After all, if you had to describe your own country to a foreigner who had never been there, you would probably spend as much time describing social mores and typical ways of acting as you would describing the landscape.

Let's consider an example. The passage quoted below concerns

Stanley Uris and his wife, and is the prelude to Stanley's suicide.

> Not that the Urises were doing so badly themselves! The suburb where they lived was a fine one, and the home which they had purchased for $87,000 in 1979 would probably now sell quickly and painlessly for $165,000 – not that she wanted to sell, but such things were good to know. She sometimes drove back from the Fox Run Mall in her Volvo (Stanley drove a Mercedes diesel – teasing him, she called it Sedanley) and saw her house, set tastefully back behind low yew hedges, and thought: Who lives there? Why, I do! Mrs Stanley Uris does!

What we learn in this short paragraph is that status symbols such as cars and houses are a big deal to the Urises. In fact, that's clearly the defining characteristic of their niche in society. But the most important feature of the quotation is that it's part of a long sequence containing almost nothing about physical experience. By the end of it, we have almost no feeling for the sights, sounds and other sensations that characterise the Urises' comfortable world. We could have heard about the peacefulness of their street, the greenness of their lawn and the softness of their leather car upholstery, but instead we learn about the couple's habits and attitudes – how proud they are to have a prestigious make of car and a sought-after address, and so on.

This description of the Urises' social environment serves a clear function within the scene as a whole – it provides a low-level, expository opening with a somewhat wandering or expansive character. And what could be more low level than a guided tour of suburban status symbols? One micro-narrative after another provides small details of highly specific events – a house price, a momentary feeling of pride in possessions, and so on. It's far from generalised, in fact it's highly specific, but it just doesn't amount to anything much. This opening phase of the scene continues for quite some time, but eventually gives way to actual character activity – Stan receiving a call from Mike. From that point onwards, we're building towards a grisly climax. But, no doubt, this is all familiar to you. It's the suspenseful scene structure that I described in the 'Toolkit for Terror' chapter. Detailed description of social setting is the first step in each instance of that template.

There is a certain amount of variation in the kind of social detail provided by different instances of the suspense scene. In contrast to the gossipy opening of the Uris scene, the information at the start of Chapter 6, section 3, covers a highly emotive subject – Eddie Corcoran's abusive upbringing.

> These shouting matches came and went in cycles. They were most common at the end of the month, when the bills came in. A policeman, called by a neighbor, might drop by once or twice when things were at their worst and tell them to tone it down. Usually that ended it. His mother was apt to give the cop the finger and dare him to take her in, but his stepdad rarely said boo.

The paragraph contains a rapid-fire sequence of social details. In no time at all, they pile up to become quite an involved story of social pathology and psychological torment: domestic violence, concerned neighbours, a cowardly abuser, a woman who is loyal in spite of being abused. How can one not feel sorrow for the child growing up in such surroundings? And this is just one short paragraph in a section that's contains page after page of these micro-narratives. The purpose is to build up massive reader sympathy for the character from scratch so that his violent end has maximum impact on us.

As we saw in the 'Toolkit for Terror' chapter, the calm opening of these scenes is always intended to set an emotional stage of some kind – a space in which the author can pull back the curtain on a horrific spectacle, like the freakshow owner in *The Elephant Man*. Accordingly, the introductory account of social setting is always configured to ensure powerful emotions are released at the climactic moment of the scene. When the dramatic high point comes and its shocking details are described with maximum vividness, we experience it as a violation of all that's human – an attack on the Urises' desire for home and comfort, or a transgression of the normal human urge to protect a child in distress.

In the two examples we've discussed so far, social setting is explored through biographical anecdotes – the Urises' big-ticket purchases and Eddie Corcoran's painful history of abuse. I'd now like to move on to a third example – Eddie Kaspbrak's visit to Neibolt Street. It's a scene that shares a number of characteristics with the suspense scenes while lacking the feeling of increasing tension. As Eddie Kaspbrak rides towards Neibolt Street, the stage is set with a rather different type of information about social setting. Here, the emphasis is on the history, politics and economics of the physical locale as we move towards his alarming encounter with a syphilitic hobo.

> His mother told him that in the old days you could catch a GS&WM passenger train at what was then Neibolt Street Station, but the passenger trains had stopped running around the time the Korean War was starting up. 'If you got on the northbound train you went to Brownsville Station,' she said, 'and from Brownsville you could catch a train that would take you all the way across Canada if you wanted, all the way to the Pacific. The southbound train would take you to Portland and then on down to Boston, and from South Station the country was yours. But the passenger trains have gone the way of the trolley lines now, I guess. No one wants to ride a train when they can just jump in a Ford and go. You may never even ride one.'

The descriptive details still have an expansive yet specific feel, just like the build up to Stanley Uris's suicide and Eddie Corcoran's slaying. In that sense, it's the same kind of calming experience before a distressing revelation. But there's another level to the way these historical, political and economic details set us up for the hobo's appearance. That is to say, they help us to understand why exactly it is that a ruined, disease-ridden man should be lurking under a house. He's there because the rail-riding lifestyle of yesteryear is fast disappearing. Like the other tramps and hobos who occasionally blow into Derry, and like the drunken trainman who throws a box of lobster to Eddie because the company made him redundant, he's high and dry in the shiny, individualistic age of the motorcar. This deft economic commentary gives a new level of richness to the scene. When the hobo appears, he's like a haunting personification of place. It illustrates an important point – that you can give the apparitions in a horror story a completely different meaning by framing them with different kinds of social reality.

Physical Setting
While the novel doesn't exactly overflow with descriptions of physical setting, it does have some very important roles to play. In fact, it appears to have been reserved for some of the most important interactions with place.

Location Overviews

The first of these roles is to give the reader a high-level overview of setting. This only occurs on a couple of occasions, but it is apparently so important that the narrative has to virtually come to a halt for it. Section 9 of Chapter 4 begins with several pages of commentary on the layout, geography and weather of Derry, focusing on the Kenduskeag Stream and the Barrens. Here is the opening paragraph.

> Like many cities, small and large, Derry had not been planned – like Topsy, it just growed. City planners never would have located it where it was in the first place. Downtown Derry was in a valley formed by the Kenduskeag Stream, which ran through the business district on a diagonal from southwest to northeast. The rest of the town had swarmed up the sides of the surrounding hills.

These pages of physical description are an immense information download with only the slenderest of connections to the novel's on-going narrative. We're eventually dovetailed back into the story, somewhat artificially, by a single sentence.

> To Ben all this geography mated with geology meant was a vague awareness that there were no more houses on his right side now; the land had dropped away.

Why is this overview description of setting so important that it has to put the brakes on the narrative like this? When it occurs, we're not far into Part 2 of the novel, and the story is entering a new phase – you could call it the fight back against 'It', or 'act 2' if you prefer. It's a moment that demands clarification of the backdrop to the story, especially the Barrens, which is a location that resonates on many thematic levels. The overview description obliges, ensuring that the reader is thoroughly familiar with the physical features of Derry, the Kenduskeag and the Barrens before the meat of the novel's narrative is served up. The passage explains what the place is, where it is and why it is. To do so, the narrative viewpoint seems to climb into a hot-air balloon and hover far above the city, travelling only through history to give the physical description an extra dimension.

Later, there's another overview of the physical aspects of Derry. Coming in Chapter 10, section 1, we can see that, once again, it occurs one of the novel's major turning points – the start of Part 3, when the reunion is occurring. This time, the viewpoint is that of Bill moving through the city on the way to the Chinese restaurant. Some of the description is Bill's own observation and some comes from the mouth of his taxi driver. But the effect is similar to the view from high above Derry in Chapter 4. It provides the same kind of survey of what Derry has become, physically, and why. It also travels through time for extra depth of meaning like the previous passage.

> 'It hasn't all changed,' Bill said. The depressing promenade of banks and parking lots was slipping behind them as they climbed Center Street. Over the hill and past the First National, they began to pick up some speed. 'The Aladdin's still there.'
> 'Yeah,' the cabbie conceded. 'But just barely' …

Neither of these physical overviews of Derry consists 100% of sensory observations. Because of their survey-like approach and historical perspectives, they tend to bring elements of social observation into their mix – like this micro-anecdote told to Bill by the taxi driver.

> 'It was the First Merchants of Penobscot County had its eye on the 'laddin. Wanted to pull it down and put up what they called a "complete banking mall." Got all the papers from the City Council, and the Aladdin was condemned. Then a bunch of folks formed a committee – folks that had lived here a long time – and they petitioned, and they marched, and they hollered, and finally they had a public City Council meeting about it, and Hanlon blew those suckers out.' The cabbie sounded extremely satisfied.

Nevertheless. The focus is mainly on physical setting, differentiating this passage from the extensive description of social setting elsewhere in the novel.

It's interesting to note that there was no such overview before the events of Part 1. Georgie's murder, Adrian Mellon's murder and telephone calls from Mike to the grown-up Losers were related without much attention being given to physical context. It's clearly Stephen King's preference to start telling his story from a low-level viewpoint, in amongst the surroundings, then pull the focus out for certain major turning points. It's not surprising that both physical overviews occur in the first half of the novel. At that time, we are still getting to know the setting and the action is not at its most intense. In the second half of the novel, as the story picks up emotional steam and we are hooked by the fates of the main characters, it's more important to maintain a low-level viewpoint, in amongst the action.

Emotional Landscapes

There are a number of scenes in which Stephen King uses sense-laden evocation of place as a way of signifying strong emotions in characters. Consider section 2 of Chapter 11, which recounts grown-up Eddie's visit to the place where he played baseball as a kid. Here's one of its passages of detailed descriptive writing.

> Standing here now, Eddie could see no trace of those rutted basepaths. Weeds had grown up through the gravel in patchy profusion. Broken soda and beer bottles twinkled here and there; in the old days, such shards of broken glass had been religiously removed. The only thing that was the same was the chainlink fence at the back of the lot, twelve feet high and as rusty as dried blood. It framed the sky in droves of diamond shapes.

On first reading, this may seem like a particularly plain piece of writing, and yet it exudes a subtle sense of menace under the nostalgia of a visit to a childhood playground. For the most part, the burden of creating a visual impression is carried by a few rather plain adjectives: 'rutted', 'patchy', 'broken'. The only fancy technique is the concluding simile, 'as rusty as dried blood'. This does instil disquiet in the reader – by making a link between the fence and physical injury. However, there's another technique that produces unsettling emotion in a simpler but less obvious way. It's that image of broken bottles. Simply by naming it, the author makes us begin to dwell on the possibility of sustaining horrible injuries during an innocent game. No matter that the bottle shards exist in a different timeframe from the kids who used to play on the field, and no matter that measures were taken to avoid such injuries back in 1958. The mere idea is enough to get readers cringing. The image is also highlighted by the use of the verb 'twinkled' – by far the most vivid and specific verb in the passage.

It's important to note that the strong emotion of disquiet is not an add-on to the physical description of the passage, it is the raison d'être for the physical description. Where there is no need to convey a powerful emotion, Stephen King simply doesn't provide that many sensory details – he tends to float along on his river of social details instead. Even in the description of the baseball field, we see an incursion of behavioural detail.

> ... in the old days, such shards of broken glass had been religiously removed.

As the story of *IT* becomes more intense, towards the conclusion, these moments of emotive physical description positively wallow in disturbing details.

> He lit one of the remaining matches and they saw a narrow tunnel stretching ahead on a downward slant. The top of this pipe was festooned with sagging cobwebs, some water-broken and hanging in shrouds. Looking at them gave Bill an atavistic chill. The floor here was dry but thick with ancient mold and what might have been leaves, fungus ... or some unimaginable droppings. Farther up he saw a pile of bones and a drift of green rags. They might once have been that stuff they called 'polished cotton,' workman's clothes. Bill imagined some Sewer Department or Water Department worker who had gotten lost, wandered down here, and been discovered ...

But even in amongst all the shiver-inducing details of cobwebs and mould, Stephen King can't help but allow the interjection of a social detail, describing how workmen of yesteryear had clothes made of polished cotton. That's indicative of the general tendency towards behavioural detail in the novel's naturalistic passages of setting description.

Horror Loci

At moments when the author introduces settings of great importance to the story of *IT*, we often feel the influence of locations that are familiar from other horror novels and movies. Although there's a stereotypical element to these special places, they're often described with convincingly naturalistic detail. In a number of cases, however, the naturalism is subsequently swept away by an eruption of anti-naturalistic supernatural detail.

Before we pursue that idea further, I'd like to introduce the concept of a 'locus'. I use this term to refer to settings in literature that are more or less formulaic. Commonly, a locus will belong to a specific genre. In many works within that genre, you will find descriptions of the same kind of setting – fleshed out with the same kind of physical details and serving the narrative in a similar way.

In a way, this technique goes to the heart of the distinction between popular novels and what might be called 'literary' novels. Literary fiction seeks to avoid the familiar and invent new effects at every turn. By contrast, popular literature seeks to revisit familiar effects and give them a new spin. Although it's common to hear literary snobs speaking disdainfully of popular novels as cliché-ridden and utterly inferior to the work of true artists questing after truth, this would have seemed an odd distinction to writers in most historical epochs and societies. From the age of Homer until the Romantic era of Western civilisation, a premium was placed on art that skilfully revisited familiar themes and settings, evoking them vividly, exploring their depths of meaning and applying that meaning to new aspects of human experience. At its best, that is what popular fiction still does, and, in my view, Stephen King is up there with the finest in his treatment of familiar themes and settings.

IT shares many of the loci (plural) common to the horror genre. By that I mean cinematic horror and literary horror, since there's a uniquely close relationship between the two media in this genre. These settings may be familiar to fans of the horror genre, but that doesn't mean Stephen King takes the opportunity to describe them in a sloppy or generalised way. In fact, they're often the focus of highly naturalistic physical description. As we'll see, two of the naturalistic physical settings that I've already described – the overview of Derry and the baseball field visited by Eddie – both correspond to common horror loci.

Let's review the full range of horror loci used in *IT*.

The Main Stage

It's important that a horror story has a limited setting within which the action will take place – a special environment that makes unusual occurrences possible. It may be cursed or blighted in some way, as with innumerable fairy-tale kingdoms that are occupied by dragons. This is very much the case with Derry. It has been infected with evil and, as it turns out, that is due to the arrival of a malign creature.

This cursed land must be defined by a boundary of some kind. That's why, early in the novel, Stephen King establishes the idea that events within Derry belong to the story, whereas anything that occurs outside the city is alien to it. Georgie's boat ceases to be of concern as soon as it leaves the town's sewage system.

> ... it was still afloat and still running on the breast of the flood when it passed the incorporated town limits of Derry, Maine, and there it passes out of this tale forever.

The author subsequently seems to weaken his own distinction between 'the main stage' and 'everywhere else' by describing many events outside of Derry – the stories of the adult Losers and their spouses. Nevertheless, the town does eventually draw in all those external characters. This not only gives an extra-sinister feel to Derry – like a whirlpool drawing bystanders in – but also gives something of the same feel to the novel and the fiction-writing process. As we saw in the quote about the little paper boat, Derry, as the main stage, is almost synonymous with the story itself.

At the end of a story containing this locus, it's important to show the reader or viewer a sign that some kind of redemption has come to the cursed land as a whole – that the dragon has been killed and fruitfulness restored. In Chapter 23, when 'It' is defeated in 1985, Derry succumbs to a major apocalyptic event reflecting the collapse of evil at its heart.

> And then, at 10:02 A.M., downtown Derry simply collapsed.

We see specific details indicating that evil no longer holds sway, like this revenant of Georgie – another boy playing with a paper boat.

> They reached the corner of Upper Main and Point Street. A kid in a red rainslicker and green rubber boots was sailing a paper boat along the brisk run of water in the gutter. He looked up, saw them looking at him, and waved tentatively.

Without such evidence of a new order, the apocalypse would not function as a moment of redemption.

Incidentally, these apocalyptic events are a perfect example of how anti-naturalistic details erupt into some of the horror loci of *IT*. This happens when a particular locus is the setting for a major plot turning point that involves the supernatural. In Chapter 23, our normal physical expectations of a city are brushed aside as events take hold that are way beyond the norms of our world – not just collapses, waterspouts and floods but exploding beer kegs, chiming clocks and other weird phenomena. The desire to convince us has been entirely replaced by the desire to thrill us. Other works in the horror genre allow the supernatural to gradually overtake and subvert the naturalistic setting. The 2001 movie *The Others* is a good example. It keeps the viewer in an almost permanent state of uncertainty about whether the setting – a highly spooky country house – really is a domain of the supernatural. But in *IT*, the impact of the supernatural is much more explosive and obvious. Accordingly, the physical descriptions take on an almost cartoon-like character.

Interestingly, this generalised description used for settings under the influence of the supernatural is in stark contrast to the detail lavished on certain moments of action associated with the supernatural – notably the vividly described deaths of Georgie, Eddie Corcoran and Stan. Although those murders obviously involve anti-naturalistic activity, the author goes to great lengths to create a convincing description. Let me explain why. I believe the author has opted to provide extreme detail in those descriptions of supernatural activity because he's attempting to achieve a specific effect – to focus the reader in on a shocking occurrence after a long, slow build-up of suspense. That effect could never be applied to the description of a setting (supernatural or otherwise) because, when the camera angle widens to take in the surroundings, the reader's attention is opened up rather than focused. So, it's only to be expected that a physical setting in the throes of a supernatural event would be described in quite generalised terms. In the case of the apocalyptic setting description in Chapter 23, the physical/supernatural details serve to give the reader emotional release after a period of close-in, dramatic action. Focus is simply not required.

The Wilderness
The name of the Barrens gives a strong clue as to its character. It's

the place where the rules of civilisation no longer apply – where comfort and order have been stripped away and you are more than likely to encounter extraordinary challenges and threats. In *Gawain and the Green Knight*, Sir Gawain travels out beyond the safe, well-lit court of King Arthur to search for his supernatural foe. Quite alone, he crosses forests, moors and mountains, dealing with wild animals and giants as he goes. In the case of the children in *IT*, the Barrens is a place where you can do battle with the forces of nature by damming a river, or clash with enemies by throwing rocks at them. You can also run into weird phenomena like the boyish masturbation experiments and the fridge full of blood-sucking creatures encountered by Bev on her travels.

Ultimately, the Barrens turns out to be the location of an entrance into the habitat of 'It', just as the wilderness turns out to be the location of the Green Knight's chapel.

The Stronghold

To continue the comparison with *Gawain and the Green Knight*, the well-lit court of Camelot also finds an equivalent in *IT*. It's the library so beloved of Ben and so devotedly supervised by Mike. Both places are luminous enclaves of order and civilisation in a cruel, disordered world. The rules of behaviour are known in the library and the values those rules enshrine are both humane and elevating.

> Ben loved the library.
> He loved the way it was always cool, even on the hottest day of a long hot summer; he loved its murmuring quiet, broken only by occasional whispers, the faint thud of a librarian stamping books and cards, or the riffle of pages being turned in the Periodicals Room, where the old men hung out, reading newspapers which had been threaded into long sticks. He loved the quality of the light, which slanted through the high narrow windows in the afternoons or glowed in lazy pools thrown by the chain-hung globes on winter evenings while the wind whined outside.

In the vicinity of strongholds, you often see evil or chaos hovering. The bully Henry Bowers and his buddies wait menacingly for Ben to emerge from the library so that they can chase him and beat him up. And, on certain occasions, evil breaks into the stronghold's safe enclosure. In *Gawain and the Green Knight*, it is, of course, the opening gambit of the story. A gigantic green figure disrupts Christmas celebrations at Camelot by challenging the knights to trade axe blows. In the 1980 movie *The Fog*, a former lighthouse – the location of a radio station with an all-night show – gets invaded by the spirits of dead sailors. In contrast to *Gawain*, they only break in towards the end of the story.

In *IT*, there are three such incursions. Firstly, Ben is haunted by 'It' during his nostalgic trip back to the library. Subsequently, the Losers are taunted by their supernatural enemy during an after-hours gathering at the library premises. Thirdly, Mike the librarian is attacked by Henry Bowers while working at night.

A Residue of Evil

In many horror stories, we see an idea that terrible events leave a residue of evil in the place where they occurred. This is what underlies Stan's terrifying experience at the standpipe in *IT*. The place was the scene of several tragic child deaths, and now the spirits of the victims apparently haunt the place. This is very similar to a memorable motif that appears in the 1998 movie *Ring* and the 2002 remake. There's a well where a young girl died, and her malevolent spirit is later seen emerging from it. Laying her to rest involves going down into the well to recover her remains.

This is a strange horror locus to employ in *IT*, given that the source of the novel's evil is not a one-off tragic event in the past. Stephen King does his best to dovetail the standpipe haunting with 'It', echoing the appearance of Pennywise in the description of the apparitions.

> Their hands lay limply at their sides, too long, too waxy-white. Depending from each finger was a small orange pompom.

But the link between the ghosts and the clown is never clarified and we're left with a nagging feeling that it doesn't quite belong in the novel. It seems to me that the residue of evil locus is not included in the story because it's particularly appropriate to the nature if 'It'. Rather, it's included in order to complete a kind of procession through all the most common horror loci in movies and literature. Stephen King is intent on drawing in as much stereotypical horror material as possible because, as we saw in the section about artistic themes, *IT* is essentially a horror novel about horror novels. In fact, the evil at its heart is a kind of personification of the horror genre. It's only to be expected, therefore, that the novel will become a sort of rattle bag of horror locations and situations – even one or two that don't seem to fit with the story's metaphysics.

The No-Go Zone

In popular fiction narratives, there's only one reason why a character would be told not to go to a particular place. It's so that we can enjoy watching them disobey and get into trouble. The archetypal example is the folk tale 'Bluebeard'. It tells how a young girl is married off to a wealthy man. After a while, she's left alone in the man's castle, having been warned not to go into one particular cellar room. Naturally, she can't control her curiosity and enters the room, discovering the mutilated remains of her husband's previous wives. Naturally, she's discovered and finds herself in big trouble.

There are a huge number of modern novels and movies in which characters are either forbidden to enter a place or warned that it would be foolish to do so. For example, in the 1999 movie *The Blair Witch Project*, the protagonists, a group of young documentary makers, are warned by a couple of fishermen not to enter a forest that has a sinister history. And in the Stephen King novel *Pet Sematary*, a doctor who has moved to a rural area discovers a place in the local woods where children bury their pets. In a dream or vision, a dead man warns him not to enter the burial place.

In Chapter 6, section 5 of *IT*, we hear about the cellarhold. It's an abandoned industrial site near the childhood home of Mike – a place with a sinister reputation as the site of some historic child killings. The boy's parents, worried about a new spate of murders, give him a clear instruction not to go to the cellarhold, and yet he can't help himself.

> Mike was not unmindful of the cellarhold and his father's warning to stay out of it; neither was he unmindful of the death that had been dealt out on this spot fifty-odd years before. He supposed that if there was a haunted place in Derry, this was it. But either in spite of that or because of it, he was determined to stay until he found something really good to take back and show his father.

Having disobeyed his parents and visited the forbidden place, Mike naturally encounters 'It'. The creature takes the form of a giant bird and he only just manages to escape with his life. It's a drama that has a strong psychological subtext, because it involves a child disobeying a parent. You don't have to know much about Freud any other theorists of the unconscious to know that conflict with fathers and mothers is at the root of personality development. The no-go zone locus lends itself to this kind of psychological expressiveness because its keynote is one of transgression against authority. In general, this locus is as much about the authority that's defied as the place itself.

The Witch's House

In section 3 of Chapter 11, Bev visits the house that was her childhood home, wondering if her estranged father is still alive. She finds a peculiar old woman living there – no relation of hers. While drinking tea and talking with her, the old woman changes into a figure like the witch in the folk story of Hansel and Gretel. The woman becomes a cackling old crone and her home becomes a cottage made of candy.

> The overhead lights were globes of hard candy. The wainscotting was caramel taffy. She looked down and saw that her shoes were leaving prints on the floorboards, which were not boards at all but slices of chocolate. The smell of candy was cloying. Oh God it's Hansel and Gretel it's the witch the one that always scared me the worst because she ate the children –
> 'You and your friends!' the witch screamed, laughing. 'You and your friends! In the cage! In the cage until the oven's hot!'

In this case, the link between a place in the novel and a well-known locus of horror is explicit – something that's recognised and openly stated by a character in the story. By now, the novel is beginning to feel like a fairground ride taking us through a sequence of well-known horror tableaus. Although this feeling is deliberately engineered by Stephen King as part of his mission to lay bare the inner workings of the horror genre, each of the loci that we visit in the novel – including this Hansel and Gretel house experience – is delivered in a bravura way that would not shame a less self-aware novel.

The Hansel and Gretel story speaks to primitive childhood fear of abandonment – like that experienced by Bev as a victim of abuse. The brother and sister of the story's title are left in the forest by their parents during a famine. They then fall into the clutches of a witch who fattens them up to eat them rather than to nurture them like a good parent. The house where the witch lives is apparently the dream home for a child – literally made of cakes and sweets – but it turns out to be an illusion. It's actually a place of death rather than comfort and care. This idea of illusory care or hospitality is the key to the witch's house locus.

Modern versions of the witch's house include the Bates Motel in the movie *Psycho*. A woman fleeing pursuers seeks refuge. The young hotel keeper seems very hospitable, but, famously, stabs her while she's in the shower.

Entrance to the Monster's Cave / Haunted House

The house at Neibolt Street is visited four times in total. First, Eddie tells in retrospect how he was exploring there and encountered a syphilitic hobo uttering sexual suggestions. Subsequently, Eddie returns and encounters a hobo figure again, although this time it's clearly 'It' in the form of the vagrant. Next, it's the turn of Bill and Richie to visit the house. They are chased away by an apparition that variously looks like a werewolf or a clown. Finally, in Chapter 18, some of the kids go to the house armed with silver bullets. Having experienced a range of terrifying and disorienting phenomena, they confront 'It' as the creature emerges from a broken toilet. The silver bullets seem to be effective, because it retreats back down the toilet.

Neibolt Street is a combination of two loci. Firstly, the weird phenomena that the kids experience on their final visit clearly correspond to the most familiar horror locus of all: the haunted house.

> Ben was standing just inside the door between the parlor and the hallway and the others were moving away from him across a space that now looked almost as big as Bassey Park … but as they moved away, they seemed to grow larger instead of smaller. The floor seemed to slope, and –
> Mike turned. 'Ben!' he called, and Ben saw alarm on his face. 'Catch up! We're losing you!' He could barely hear the last word. It trailed away as if the others were being swept off on a fast train.

116

Suddenly terrified, he began to run. The door behind him swept shut with a muffled bang. He screamed … and something seemed to sweep through the air just behind him, ruffling his shirt. He looked back but there was nothing there.

Buildings that either seem to be attacking the occupants, or which are home to a hostile presence, are ubiquitous in movies and literature. The distortions of space described above are reminiscent of the set created for the 1963 movie *The Haunting*, with its weird angles and low ceilings. Another notable example is *The Amityville Horror* – a book that was adapted twice as a movie. It follows a very typical pattern: a couple move to a new house and are terrified by phenomena such as swarms of flies, slamming doors and a ghostly figure.

Almost unfailingly, haunted house settings turn out to be a variation on another locus: the residue of evil. In all versions of *The Amityville Horror*, and in both versions of The Haunting (1963 and 1999) it's discovered that the house was the scene of violent deaths in the past. The thing that sets the haunted house locus apart is that it focuses specifically on the subversion of domestic security. Everything that's cosy and familiar about the idea of home is turned into a source of fear. One of the finest examples is the moment in a *Hammer House of Horror* episode from 1980 called 'The House That Bled to Death'. During the scene in question, a small group of children are gathered around a table for a party when a pipe bends itself away from the wall and sprays the table with blood. In a similar way, during the final Neibolt Street episode, a family of rats are found in a drawer.

So much for the haunted houses. Now let's consider the second locus that Neibolt Street seems to conform to: the entrance to the monster's cave.

If you've never read Joseph Campbell's seminal work about story structure, *The Hero's Journey*, I suggest you do so. It describes a basic pattern for tales of adventure that is rooted in ancient myth and legend. In summary, the pattern involves a hero leaving the ordinary world and entering a special world – a process that involves conflicts and the sealing of alliances. Once in the special world, the hero approaches the entrance to a cave where some kind of enemy dwells. Initially, they don't enter the cave. Instead, they gather around them a group of friends and plot how to overcome various guardians of the cave.

Of course, this locus need not literally involve a cave entrance. In the 1982 movie *Poltergeist*, it's the television. Behind its screen are the supernatural beings that have abducted a young girl. With no idea how to get in there and retrieve her, the girl's family turn to a paranormal investigator for help. In modern horror stories, approaching the cave is often more about tackling some problematic aspect of psychology, as in the book and movie of *The Silence of the Lambs*. FBI investigator Clarice Starling must open up to Hannibal Lector about a secret trauma before he will help her find the serial killer Buffalo Bill.

Both types of cave-approaching experience – literal and psychological – are found in the encounter at Neibolt Street. The literal cave entrance is a broken toilet from which 'It' emerges in the form of a werewolf. The psychological cave entrance is every single trauma suffered by the kids at the hands of 'It' or the creature's human lackeys. The key to attacking both problems is the same: work as a group. The previous visits to the house were rather half-baked affairs in small groups and without much of a plan. Once there is a group of friends who believe one another's stories about 'It' and understand one another's suffering, the attack can be pressed home much more successfully.

Neibolt Street and the preceding locus, the Marsh Residence, are two more examples of settings that are suddenly and overwhelmingly affected by supernatural forces. Once again, the idea of providing convincing detail is thrown to the winds – replaced by a cascade of thrilling but two-dimensional phenomena. Here's a passage from the description of Neibolt Street in section 8 of Chapter 18.

> Abruptly the corridor seemed to elongate. The ceiling rose and then began to diminish above them like some weird rocket. The doors grew with the ceiling, pulled up like taffy. The faces of the elves grew long and became alien, their eyes bleeding black holes.

The points of description are rattled off one after another, and there's an emotive yet unspecific quality to phrases such as 'like some weird rocket' and 'became alien'. They express the disorienting, hallucinatory quality of the surroundings rather than creating a convincing visual impression. Contrast this with the naturalistic details used to describe the exterior of the house before the supernatural influence really explodes into the scene.

> The leaves under the porch crackled and puffed up a sour old smell. Ben wrinkled his nose. Had he ever smelled fallen leaves like these? He thought not. And then an unpleasant idea struck him. They smelled the way he imagined a mummy would smell, just after its discoverer had levered open its coffin: all dust and bitter an ancient tannic acid.

The quotation dwells on a single phenomenon – the leaves – and uses two different senses to describe them – sound and smell. Sure, the supernatural is there, but only in the background.

The Hunting Ground
In horror stories, there is an inherent need to transport the main characters from the world of the ordinary, where everything is predictable and safe, to the land of the extraordinary, where terrifying things are likely to happen. This transition is often marked by events that signify the crossing of boundaries. It may also occur with the help of unusual means of transport. There are many moments in a story when this can happen, but, if nowhere else, it will definitely happen in the opening stages, when a protagonist is entering the main stage. As you will appreciate, this is a key event that makes the rest of the horror narrative possible. The transition may also happen when a character is approaching any of the other loci described above.

Often, the transition is no more than a brief moment in the story when a boundary is crossed and the rules suddenly change for the characters. An example is the moment when Bill rides with Richie towards Neibolt Street for one of their visits.

> They sped along, the houses thinning out a little now, the streets crossing Witcham at longer intervals.
> 'Hi-yo Silver!' Bill yelled
> …
> Silver bumped over one set of train tracks, then another.

There's a special mode of transport – Bill's bicycle – and there's a sense that the two of them are passing through boundaries as they ride out to a remote part of Derry – the buildings are thinning and they cross the important social boundary of a railway track. This journey finds many parallels in movies and literature – characters making transitions from a relatively ordinary world to one horror locus or another. Think, for example, of Jonathan Harker's wild ride to Count Dracula's castle. He travels into an ever more savage landscape, rising higher into the mountains. At first, the means of transport is a public carriage, but then Harker is picked up by the Count's own horse-drawn caliche. They travel on towards the castle accompanied by wolves.

The kind of transition described above is not a locus in its own right. Rather, it's a feature of loci in general and how they're introduced into the narrative. However, there are certain moments of transition in horror narratives that are so important they're given their own physical setting. I refer to such settings as 'hunting grounds' because they remind me of a particular motif in medieval literature – the idea that you can encounter something strange or terrifying while chasing quarry through the forest. In the famous tale of 'The Three Living and the Three Dead', of which there are many medieval tellings, a group of three kings are out hunting when they encounter a grisly spectacle: three walking, talking dead men. The animated corpses proceed to tell the hunters that they too were kings once and enjoyed worldly pleasures like hunting. The moral, of course, is that the living should remember they won't be around forever.

In modern horror and thriller literature, the hunting ground has its equivalent – settings where people wander off the beaten track and into an adventure. One example is *Watchers* by Dean Koontz. Its central character is out on a trek in the forest when he encounters two strange creatures: a dog with unnaturally high levels of intelligence and a monstrous beast of some kind, which gets away. It's a weird encounter that sets a complex narrative in motion.

In *IT*, we see an example of a hunting ground that's part of the man-made environment rather than the natural world. I'm referring to the baseball pitch improvised by kids in 1958 and revisited by Eddie in 1985. I consider it a hunting ground because it's a place where people get carried away with a physical activity and have an unexpected encounter. Specifically, Eddie recalls how Belch Huggins once hit the ball out over the fence, forcing him to go and search for it in the Barrens. Eddie's 1985 self stands in the same place gazing out over the fence towards the Barrens when he has a supernatural encounter.

> 'Come on down and play, Eddie,' the voice on the other side of the fence said, and Eddie realized with a fainting sort of horror that it was the voice of Belch Huggins, who had been murdered in the tunnels under Derry in August of 1958.

But, in general, this particular locus is not strongly affected by supernatural forces. That is the reason why we see such close attention to convincing details like the glass scattered on the pitch – as mentioned earlier – and an absence of the cartoon-like descriptions associated with Neibolt Street and elsewhere. It's a perfect example of how a horror locus can be somewhat stereotypical and yet entirely naturalistically described.

Period Setting

So far, we've concentrated on the social and physical aspects of setting in *IT*, but there's another important dimension to the novel: time. In fact, one of the most characteristic features of the story is the way it takes place in two timeframes – 1958 and 1985 – flipping back and forth between them. The transitions between these two periods don't always occur in a predictable sequence, and the reader can't always rely on clear signals like chapter headings to tell them which timeframe they're in. So, a sense of period is conveyed almost exclusively through details of speech and setting.

We saw earlier how Stephen King tailors the speech of characters to a particular period. The exchanges between the kids are especially redolent of playground banter between middle-class boys and girls in 1950s America.

> 'Oh shit and Shinola!' he yelled, dismayed.

But description of physical and social setting is just as important an indicator of timeframe. Period details abound in the 1957 sections, and, as you might expect, Chapter 1 is particularly thick with them. In addition to mentioning 1957 in the heading and twice more in the opening paragraphs, the author supplies a steady flow of behaviours, environments and objects that clearly belong to 1950s America. It all helps to get us tuned in to the feel of that particular historical moment.

> Bill had made the boat beside which George now ran. He had made it sitting up in bed, his back propped against a pile of pillows, while their mother played Für Elise on the piano in the parlor
>
> …
>
> 'Can I do some?' George asked.
>
> 'Okay. Just don't get any on the blankets or Mom'll kill you.'
>
> George dipped his finger into the paraffin, which was now very warm but no longer hot, and began to spread it along the other side of the boat.
>
> …
>
> Every now and then someone went crazy and killed a lot of people – sometimes Chet Huntley told about such things on the evening news – and of course there were Commies

Making paper boats and waterproofing them with paraffin; a mother playing the piano in the parlour; blankets on the bed; shootings and Communists on the evening news. It's USA, 1957.

Takeaway

- The dense naturalistic description of setting in *IT* focuses on social details, reserving extensive physical description for specific contexts.
  - o Social setting
    - Beliefs and behaviours are just as important as physical environment when describing setting.
    - One context in which social setting can be useful is the opening of a scene that builds up from everyday details to an action climax
    - Details of social setting used in this way should not be generalised rather streams of detailed mini-anecdotes.
    - This opening to the scene should set the stage for a certain type of emotional experience at the violent climax.
    - Depending on the context, it may be most appropriate to begin such scenes with either biographical details of the viewpoint character or historical / political / economic details of the location.

○ Physical setting
- Provide a high-level physical overview of physical setting at the start of novel parts.
- Evoke the emotional state of the viewpoint character through physical details of setting.
- Include horror loci – location types commonly found in novels and movies.
  - The main stage
    - ○ Blighted land oppressed by a monster.
    - ○ Supernatural forces influence the description of Derry in an explosive way at the climax of the novel – the details become 'cartoon-like'.
  - The wilderness
    - ○ The domain of adventures and location of the monster's lair.
  - The stronghold
    - ○ A bastion of civilisation – invaded by evil.
  - A residue of evil
    - ○ Terrible events in the past have left traces in a physical location.
  - The no-go zone
    - ○ Heroes defy authority by entering a place and get into trouble as a result.
  - The witch's house
    - ○ A place of illusory hospitality.
  - Entrance to the monster's cave / Haunted house
    - ○ Joseph Campbell's concept of an approach to a monster's lair.
    - ○ A variation on the 'residue of evil' locus.
    - ○ Descriptions of Neibolt Street

and the Marsh Residence transition from naturalistic to cartoon-like details as supernatural forces take hold.

- The hunting ground
  - When you're carried away with some physical activity the uncanny may be encountered.
  - A good example of dense, naturalistic description in a horror locus.
  - Period setting
    - There are many physical and speech-related details that evoke period.

5. NARRATIVE STRUCTURE

'Haiku was good poetry, Ben felt, because it was structured poetry.'
– Stephen King, *IT*

In this chapter, I'll be taking two different approaches to analysing the narrative structure of *IT*. The first approach focuses on scenes, chapters and other subdivisions. It seeks to understand the effects that can be created by playing with the shape, content and sequence of those building blocks. The second approach focuses on plot, subplot and other narrative features that extend through the novel, running in parallel. It considers the shape and content of those features as well as analysing the way they intertwine and intersect.

Building Blocks

One of the most characteristic features of *IT* is the way it has been constructed using a relatively complex system of subdivisions – namely parts, chapters, sections, interludes and an epilogue. This is not just intended to give the reader a convenient stopping place when they decide to put the book down. The multi-level structure helps to create a story that feels robust. Think of a novel as a bridge. If an engineer simply took a load of girders and bolted their ends together, it wouldn't make for a very effective river crossing. The girders need to be built up into bigger structures, which are in turn connected together to form a stable bridge. Just so with

125

writing a novel. If you're spanning a very large gap – more than 1000 pages of fantastical events in this case – you need to be sure that the individual events are built up into convincing scenes, the scenes into satisfying chapters, the chapters into monolithic story parts and the story parts into a novel that feels complete and satisfying. Let's look at the detail of Stephen King's story engineering in *IT*.

Parts

The novel consists of five parts – you could think of them as acts like those in a play. Five-act stories are very common in the theatre – at least in historical drama. The form was first described by the Roman poet Horace in his *Ars Poetica* and became a convention of Roman drama. Because of that classical pedigree, early editors of Shakespeare's plays imposed a five-act structure on them, which the bard himself probably wouldn't have recognised. Nevertheless, five-act structure has become a talking point of narrative studies largely on the back of its association with Shakespeare. This was solidified by the 19th-century literary critic Gustav Freytag, whose 1863 study *Die Technik des Dramas* used Shakespearean and classical examples to describe the five-act form. It has become a well-known and influential document in the study of story.

Hollywood screenwriting – in many ways the cutting edge of popular culture – has never had much truck with the five-act structure. Instead, it went back to an even earlier authority than Horace for its narrative conventions – Aristotle's description of narrative structure in *Poetics*. His beguilingly simple observation that a story needs a beginning, a middle and end is the basis of the three-act structure, and it's this approach that became standard in Hollywood screenwriting. Contemporary popular novelists – who have learned a great deal from the movie industry in recent decades – also tend to go for three acts.

Given the modern preference for the three-act structure, it's highly significant that *IT* uses a less fashionable five-act structure. You could argue that the three-act structure described in seminal works like *Save the Cat* by Blake Snyder is in fact that five-act structure in disguise (see the appendix on this subject). But Stephen King positively flaunts his five-act structure by formally breaking the text into five named 'parts'. There's no way it could be mistaken for three acts. And you don't have to stretch your imagination too much to see a correspondence between Freytag's theoretical framework and the plot of *IT*. Here's the structure outlined by Freytag.

1. Exposition: The characters, settings and main challenge are introduced.
2. Rising action: The characters struggle with obstacles as they deal with the main challenge.
3. Climax: A high point of tension that represents a major turning point.
4. Falling action: Consequences felt, twists revealed, unknown details become known.
5. Denouement: The resolution of the main challenge.

And here's my analysis of the five parts of *IT*.

1. Exposition: Encounters with 'It' in 1958 and 1985. The heroes are called to action.
2. Rising action: The heroes' recover memories of their 1958 encounters with 'It'.
3. Climax: The heroes come together in 1985 to destroy 'It'.
4. Falling action: The heroes' initial attack on 'It' in 1958 (at Neibolt Street).
5. Denouement: Final attacks on 'It' in 1958 and 1985 (in the tunnels).

While the action of the rising action is in 1958 – before the heroes' call to action in the exposition section – its positioning within the narrative structure allows it to perform the role of rising action. In other words, we perceive the traumatic experiences of the Losers' childhoods as a set of obstacles involved in getting to grips with the main challenge.

At first glance, you might think it's pushing things a little too far to describe the reunion in the Chinese restaurant as a climax of tension. It's certainly a major turning point, but tension isn't one of its chief characteristics – at least if you're thinking of tension in terms of suspense or high stakes. The reunion scenes focus more on the deepening of relationships and an act of commitment to the main challenge (although the scary fortune-cookie episode is bolted on at the end). But this would be a misunderstanding of the kind of tension that Freytag has in mind. Let's consider one of Shakespeare's plays that he uses to illustrate his five-act structure. This may help to clarify how the act-three climax might work in practice.

Othello:

1. Exposition: A legal case against Othello reveals widespread resentment of his marriage to Desdemona.
2. Rising action: Othello demotes Cassio, who is persuaded to appeal to Desdemona for help.
3. Climax: Othello is persuaded that Desdemona may be guilty of infidelity.
4. Falling action: Othello watches for signs of Desdemona's infidelity with Cassio
5. Denouement: Othello kills Desdemona.

As you can see, the climax section contains an episode that's not really characterised by high-stakes action or suspense. The tension is instead linked to a moral change that reorients the central character towards a new course of action and entails high emotion. The same can certainly be said of the Chinese restaurant scenes in *IT*. The Losers haven't communicated for many years. They're also opening up to one another about the most troubled areas of their lives. And, most importantly, they're making a definitive commitment to the action of the second half.

You should also not be misled by the customary description of act four (in English) as the 'falling action.' The term doesn't imply a falling off of intensity. If anything, it seems to imply a quickening pace and increasing emotion as the terrible consequences of the climax work themselves out. There's an appalling inevitability about Othello's progress towards ruin in the fourth act. Similarly, the Losers are on a collision course with 'It' from the reunion onwards. Admittedly, Part 4 occurs in 1958 – 27 years before the reunion in the Chinese restaurant – but it still performs a 'falling action' function, because it shows the Losers taking concrete steps towards the goal of destroying 'It'.

Aside from any direct inspiration Freytag and his historical exemplars may have had on the writing of *IT*, I think there's also an indirect connection. Dividing the story of *IT* into five parts seems to lift it out of the normal constraints of the Hollywood-style three-act drama, giving it a Rolls-Royce feeling of expansiveness and prestige. It feels as though you're engaging with a story that's on a different plain from the generality of movies and thriller novels. This is a novel that exhibits none of the storytelling economy achieved by the screenwriting industry and documented in hundreds of how-to books for writers. Instead, it splurges out into multiple acts, which are separated by interludes and capped by an epilogue. You sense the ghost of Shakespeare conferring a blessing on the whole stately edifice.

One fascinating feature of each of the novel's parts is the way Stephen King adds quotations to each of their title pages. There are also quotes at the start of the interludes that conclude each part. Significantly, the quotes include material from highbrow sources, such as the poem *Paterson* by William Carlos Williams, but alongside lowbrow sources such as pop song lyrics – all clearly selected for their appropriateness to the story content. There's an evident desire to expand the reach of *IT*, encompassing more and more cultural territory and finding additional ways to express meaning. It's entirely in keeping with the expansiveness of the five-act structure.

Before we move on to a detailed discussion of chapters in *IT*, let's briefly consider how the novel's parts are built up using chapter building blocks.

There's an extremely variable number of chapters per part – ranging from three to six. The lesson here is that it's important not to get hung up on neatness of design when you consciously create a story as a sequence of acts. They don't have to be anything like the same length. Stephen King has chosen to make his exposition and climax acts briefer than the others.

Within one of the parts of *IT* we see a clear design principle at work. You could hardly fail to notice that the chapters in Part 2 have similar subject matter – they all focus on a single character as they remember some traumatic event from their past. Whilst it would be strange and a little tedious if all the parts of the novel had an ordering principle, it can be effective if used in a limited way. I believe the ordering of Part 2 performs two important functions. Firstly, it makes the reader feel that Part 2 is distinctly different from Part 1. This accentuates the act structure of the novel.

Secondly, the orderly sequences of chapters create a mesmerising rhythm rather like that of a fairy tale. We're all aware of how things generally happen in threes in fairy tales – three billy goats, three little pigs, three bears etc. This repetition creates a mild form of suspense as you anticipate the moment when a repeating formula will give way to something new. While things don't happen in threes in *IT*, the rhythm is similarly hypnotic, drawing us in just like children hearing a story. It's no surprise that Stephen King chooses to give his text something of the flavour of a fairy tale. It's a very important aspect of the novel's thematic content, as we've seen.

Chapters

The first thing to note about the chapters in *IT* is that there's a division of labour. In addition to the main story chapters, the novel incorporates interludes and an epilogue. We'll consider them one at a time.

The main story chapters vary considerably in length. The shortest is 17 pages, the longest 130 pages (at around 300 words per page). There is also a variable number of chapters in each part of the novel. Diversity and unpredictability is the rule, suggesting that Stephen King is generally pragmatic about the design of chapters, allowing story needs to dictate their form and quantity.

Although many of their formal characteristics vary, each of the chapters in *IT* represents a substantial step in the novel's main story – a chunk of narrative that's clearly defined, sizeable and contains one or more important turning points. The scope and focus of every chapter is, in fact, stated in its descriptive title, although sometimes a little poetically or indirectly. After all, why would you want to give away the major plot development. The title of Chapter 17, for example, is 'Another One of the Missing: The Death of Patrick Hockstetter'. As per the title, the chapter is about a set of ghastly events that Bev witnesses at the city dump, culminating in the death of the nauseating Hockstetter, who is one of the local bullies. However, the title avoids revealing the most important thing about Patrick Hockstetter's death – the fact that Bev followed a trail of his blood to the hiding place of 'It'. That is only discovered in the penultimate section of the chapter.

Some chapters are closely associated with a particular character – and I'm not just referring to the ordered chapters of Part 2 that I discussed above. In Chapter 17 for example, it's Bev who provides

WRITE LIKE STEPHEN KING

the subject matter and the viewpoint. She's wandering around the dump practising with her slingshot when she witnesses the local bullies playing grubby games. Just about everything in the chapter is seen from her concealed vantage point. There is a digression into Patrick Hockstetter's sadistic backstory, which couldn't possibly be shown from Bev's viewpoint, but we come back to the dump to witness Patrick's death at the refrigerator and to see Bev follow a trail of blood to the tunnel entrance.

Some chapters that are closely associated with a single character helpfully name that character in the title. In Chapter 16, for example, the title character is Eddie. The action of the chapter duly focuses on Eddie's fake aspirator, and we follow his viewpoint as he confronts the pharmacist and his mother for deceiving him. But naming a character is by no means the rule in chapters with a focal character. For example, Mike is the focus of Chapter 14. It describes how he's received into the Losers Club and how he experienced terrifying encounters with 'It' at the library and the cellarhold. We also hear about his album full of old pictures haunted by Pennywise. However, Mike is not mentioned in the chapter title.

Other chapters in *IT* focus on group activity rather than the activities of a specific character. As a result, they tend to pass the viewpoint around quite promiscuously. I discussed a technique of this kind in the 'Character' chapter above. We saw how, in the Chapter 7 account of the dam building, the narration sometimes occupies a shared viewpoint space between characters. But that's not an isolated case. We see similar forms of head hopping used in other chapters that focus on group identity – in Chapter 10, for example, which describes the reunion dinner at the Chinese restaurant. Section 4 clearly begins in Mike's head.

'The murders have started again,' Mike said flatly.
He looked up and down the table, and then his eyes fixed on Bill's.

And we implicitly remain in Mike's head for most of the section because he dominates the dialogue. However, at various points we shift to Bill's viewpoint – for example, at the very end of the section.

Bill looked up at Mike grimly. He had been bewildered and

frightened; now he felt the first stirrings of anger. He was glad. Angry was not such a great way to feel, but it was better than the shock, better than the miserable fear. 'Is that written in what I think it's written in?'

We can tell we're in his head because we have direct access to his emotions.

Chapter 11 also uses viewpoint shifts to dramatise issues of group identity – but in a slightly different way. Coming immediately after the reunion, this part of the novel is still suffused with a sense of the Losers' rediscovered kinship. Although we don't see the group together, they're all clearly undergoing the same personal journey. Successive sections of the chapter focus on a different member of the group as they visit a significant place from their childhood. Naturally, there's a new viewpoint for each personal story. This regular shift to the head of a new group member creates a sense of kinship in separation.

Incidentally, it seems to me that the sections of Chapter 11 have an orderliness that's very similar to the orderliness of the Chapters in Part 2. In both cases, we see the focus shift from group member to group member as each individual undergoes a similar experience. In both cases, this repetitiousness helps to create a reassuring but moderately suspenseful rhythm.

We now move on to interludes. An interlude chapter occurs after each of the five parts of the novel. Their difference from the other chapters around them is immediately clear, since they largely consist of anecdotes about Derry in years gone by, showing how 'It' has operated in the past. There's literally nothing in the interludes that's essential to the main story. All five of them could be edited out and, although the novel would be less rich in texture, the story would be perfectly understandable. The author reinforces the sense of difference by creating an illusion that the interludes are extracts from a book being written by Mike Hanlon. Consequently, they have a viewpoint that's distant from the action and a tone of voice that's distinctively academic. Outside of the interludes themselves, there is scarcely any mention of the fact that Mike is working on a book, further enhancing sense of separation between the ordinary chapters and the interludes.

The separateness and difference of the five interludes serves two functions. Firstly, readers find variety of texture refreshing in a long novel. Secondly, the violent and highly public nature of the historical anecdotes increases the stakes of the novel without taking the focus away from the seven heroes. I'm thinking of terrifying episodes like the mass murder of black servicemen in the second interlude. With forces like that regularly rearing their head in a society, it seems likely that periodic outbreaks of murder and mayhem will curse Derry for centuries to come unless 'It' can be destroyed.

In spite of the obvious difference of the interludes, the author is careful to create a few points of connection with the rest of the novel. Firstly, the content of the interludes includes a certain amount of discursive commentary on the significance of the main story chapters. For example, Mike describes his doubts over the wisdom of calling the other Losers back to Derry in the first interlude.

> If it has started again, I will call them. I'll have to. But not yet. It's too early anyway. Last time it began slowly and didn't really get going until the summer of 1958. So … I wait. And fill up the waiting with words in this notebook

In a very long and complex novel, these discursive moments are important opportunities to step back and reinforce the reader's understanding of events and themes.

Secondly (and somewhat unexpectedly) the historical anecdotes that mostly fill the interludes also create connections with the main narrative. Although there are no direct links to the experiences of the Losers, the historical tales contribute to our understanding of those experiences on the level of theme. For example, in the story about Maine loggers in the fourth interlude, the forest is compared to a virgin undergoing a rape. This brings to mind some of the sexual abuse issues associated with Bev's story.

> It was their grandfathers and great-grandfathers who actually spread the legs of the forests north of Derry and Bangor and raped those green-gowned virgins with their axes and peaveys. They cut and slashed and strip-timbered and never looked back. They tore the hymen of those great forests open when Grover Cleveland was President and had pretty well finished the job by the time Woodrow Wilson had his stroke. These lace-ruffled ruffians raped the great woods, impregnated them with a litter of slash and junk spruce, and

changed Derry from a sleepy little ship-building town into a booming honky-tonk where the ginmills never closed and the whores turned tricks all night long.

In the same interlude, we hear about someone escaping a slaughter via a whole in a toilet, recalling the werewolf's means of escape from the Neibolt Street house. These moments may seem to be only tangentially related to the rest of the novel, but the thematic resonances are strong.

The epilogue is a narrative section rather like the main story chapters. But its function is to deepen and conclude the themes of the story rather than to add anything new in terms of conflict and resolution. The central struggle of the novel – with 'It' – is over, and all that remains is to help us put that victory in perspective. Old traumas and old loves have been remembered and apparently resolved. Some of the Losers seem destined to continue repeating the mistakes of the past, but Bill and Audra have apparently found a way of accepting the past and living for today – as the wild therapeutic ride on Bill's childhood bicycle indicates. Because of this thematic emphasis, the events of the epilogue occur quite a while after the climactic action of the story (in terms of story time). That gives them their own feeling of separateness and difference – they're taking place in a calm, reflective space rather than a hectic, event-driven space.

Sections

The decision to subdivide chapters into numbered sections is what allows some of the novel's chapters to reach a considerable length – up to 130 pages. The sections work like building blocks – self-contained episodes that can be combined into quite elaborate narratives. In themselves, the sections are extremely variable in terms of length and the number within a chapter. One consists of just three sentences, but others can be as long as 30 pages (at around 300 words per page).

Most often, a chapter section in *IT* contains a single scene. That's not a hard and fast rule, but it's a close correlation. Before I go on to explore that statement further, allow me to offer a simple definition of a scene. I consider it to be a piece of continuous action with the same set of characters in the same location, revolving around a single conflict or motivation that's resolved either satisfactorily or unsatisfactorily by the end. By that definition, a reasonable number of the novel's chapter sections consist of just one scene. For example, section 2 of Chapter 17 contains a single episode that meets all those criteria. The characters and the location are clear (Bev is at the dump watching the bullies light their farts), the conflict is Bev's struggle to satisfy her curiosity without being seen and we are shown that she is successful in doing so. The scene and the section end there.

Some sections that contain a single scene emphasise their unity of purpose by adopting a title describing their key character and main action. For example, the title of Chapter 3, section 1, is 'Stanley Uris Takes a Bath'. Interestingly, it's mainly in Chapter 3 that we see this title technique used. Perhaps the author was anxious to provide readers with a period of clearly defined action after two chapters in which a great deal of discontinuity occurred. Changes of viewpoint, location, timeframe and action sequence are rife throughout chapters 1 and 2, but rarer in Chapter 3.

But nothing is as simple as it seems. There are some interesting exceptions to the one-section-one-scene model in *IT*. For one thing, some sections contain the first part of a scene that cuts off and then resumes in a later section. An example of this would be sections 4, 5 and 6 of Chapter 6. In section 4, Mike Hanlon (as a kid) is wandering around in a park when he finds a knife. He suspects that it belongs to a recently murdered boy, and this reminds Mike of something that happened to him a while ago. In section 5, we hear all about Mike's earlier experience – 'It' appearing in the form of a giant bird. But then, in section 6, we return to Mike in the park. He disposes of the knife.

The Epilogue chapter also has sections that only contain part of a scene. But, in this case, it's not done in order to abandon a scene and pick it up again after a digression as described above. Rather, the Epilogue is mostly one continuous scene – Bill and Audra at Mike's home, trying to heal her catatonic state. The sections are more or less arbitrary subdivisions. They seem designed simply to break up the flow of the narrative. The effect is totally in keeping with the role of the epilogue as a thematic meditation rather than a means of pushing the plot forward.

There are some sections in *IT* that contain multiple consecutive scenes, but they are few and far between. They tend be the product of a natural shift in dramatic emphasis from one motivation to another – but within a continuous piece of action. For example, Chapter 19, section 1 begins with the whole of the Losers' Club drawing together and feeling a surge of supernatural group power. But the section ends with a romantic moment between Bill and Bev as they rekindle their childhood attraction.

IT may not have many consecutive scenes within a single section, but various sections do contain scenes that make a brief digression into a mini-scene before resuming where they left off. Naturally, there's always a sound pretext for the digression, such as a moment of recollection or storytelling. For example, in section 9 of Chapter 9, the kids share morbid stories that they've heard about the standpipe. These are quite highly developed accounts that almost take us out of the kids' viewpoints into a separate narrative with a distinct atmosphere and voice.

> Stan stopped laughing first and looked at Eddie intently.
> 'Tell me what you know about the Standpipe,' he said.
> Eddie started, but both Ben and Beverly also contributed. The Derry Standpipe stood on Kansas Street, about a mile and a half west of downtown, near the southern edge of the Barrens …

From the words 'The Derry Standpipe' onwards, we are immersed in a new narrative. There are occasional moments of recollection that it's a story being told by someone – scraps of dialogue and a phrase such as 'Ben called them'. But, for the most part, we are in a different time and place for several paragraphs – until Bev takes over with her own addition to the story at 'I heard it from this kid Vic Crumly'.

One or two sections in *IT* don't really relate to any scene structure at all. Chapter 6, section 1, stands out from its surroundings because it consists of just three short sentences.

> They weren't all found. No; they weren't all found. And from time to time wrong assumptions were made.

The three statements refer to an outbreak of child murder in Derry. In the ensuing sections, we go on to hear about the detail of one of those murders, but this abrupt opening to the chapter is an initial slap round the face – a challenge to Derry's indifference. Essentially, the function of this section is to set the emotional tone for the chapter rather than push the narrative forward.

Scenes

Let me begin by reiterating my working definition of a scene: it's a piece of continuous action with the same set of characters in the same location, revolving around a single conflict or motivation that's resolved either satisfactorily or unsatisfactorily by the end. Most storytelling media use a basic building block of this kind, and its certainly the fundamental dramatic unit of *IT* – even if scenes are occasionally split up by section breaks, as described above.

However, one of the most important steps in developing a distinctive voice as a novelist or screenwriter is to develop a characteristic approach to scenes – a structure that honours the basic requirements of a scene but also has the author's personal stamp on it. The movies of Quentin Tarantino, for example, are full of scenes that are long and heavy on dialogue, with subject matter that's at odds with our expectations of character. A typical scene in the novels of Frederick Forsyth is also long, but with very little dialogue. It tends to be a slow, steady, detailed account of micro-actions taken by the viewpoint character.

In *IT*, there's also a characteristic scene type. I refer to it as the 'funnel'. It's structured as follows.

1. Exposition
2. Character activity
3. Conflict initiation
4. Conflict drawing on the exposition
5. Conflict resolution

Section 4 of Chapter 9 is a good example. Initially, the scene displays no particular conflict or motivated action, just a lot of circumstantial information about Derry and its history.

> The southwest was where the land fell away steeply to the area that was known in Derry as the Barrens. The Barrens – which were anything but barren – were a messy tract of land about a mile and a half wide by three miles long.

After several pages of this, we see the first sign of motivated character activity.

> To Ben all this geography mated with geology meant was a vague

awareness that there were no more houses on his right side now; the land had dropped away. A rickety whitewashed railing, about waist-high, ran beside the sidewalk, a token gesture of protection. He could faintly hear running water; it was the sound-track to his continuing fantasy.

He paused and looked out over the Barrens, still imagining her eyes, the clean smell of her hair.

A solitary Ben is yearning for Bev. Very soon, this motive gives way to conflict – he's plucked from his reverie by the local bullies laughing at him.

A hand fell on Ben's shoulder, and he screamed.

As the situation develops, the relevance of the earlier circumstantial detail becomes apparent – Ben is chased out into the Barrens by the bullies and our knowledge of the size and wildness of that place helps us picture the scene and appreciate that Ben is being pushed further away from help and deeper into trouble.

Ben pushed with his legs, adding his own force to Henry's. He hit the white-washed railing between Kansas Street and the drop into the Barrens ... there was a cracking, splintering sound from the railing.

Our concern for Ben climaxes and is relieved slightly when he makes a successful fightback.

He lumbered forward, squashy Keds spatting in the shallow water, and kicked Henry squarely in the balls.

The remainder of this section is a bridge to the next scene – an encounter with kids building a dam in the Barrens.

This is a very typical scene profile in *IT*: a movement from general information to more and more focused activity. We previously saw one highly specialised variant of it in those suspenseful scenes described in the 'Toolkit for Terror' chapter. You'll recall that Stephen King often builds up to a moment of intense horror by taking us through three distinct stages.

1. Normal human events or information about setting.

2. Ambiguous details that could be supernatural but could equally be down to an overactive imagination on the part of the viewpoint character.
3. 'It' reveals itself openly and clearly.

It's easy to see how this maps onto the funnel pattern. But, as Ben's run-in with the bullies at the Barrens shows, it's not just horror scenes that are given the funnel treatment in *IT*. Another (much briefer) example occurs in Chapter 4, section 1. It has quite a different twist on the five-stage template. To start with, we find ourselves looking through the viewpoint of a member of cabin staff on an aircraft. The exposition is carried out as she describes her impression of a passenger who is obviously Ben.

> The lanky man's eyes are on hers, but they are not seeing her. They do not move. They are perfectly glazed. Surely they are the eyes of a dead man.

You could say that the character activity stage begins when we swap from the air stewardess's viewpoint to Ben's.

> She hurries away, glad to be rid of that gaze – that deadly, almost hypnotic gaze.
> Ben Hanscom turns his head to the window and looks out.

Ben is in the throes of a conflict – an internal struggle. He's trying to bring some memory into focus.

> He closed his eyes. The air around him was full of chimes. The plane rocked and rolled and bumped and the air was full of chimes. Chimes? No ... bells. It was bells ...

As he struggles with his memory, it becomes clear why he was looking like a dead man from the stewardess's point of view. The past has some very uncomfortable associations.

> He thinks; My God, I am being digested by my own past.

But, finally, the conflict is resolved as he tunes into a memory from 1958.

... and suddenly he is here, here in June of 1958;

The funnel design may be a particularly characteristic feature of *IT*, but it's not an all-purpose tool. We see many other scene profiles in the novel, each serving a different dramatic purpose. For example, Chapter 3, section 6 is really the opposite of a funnel. It starts at a dramatic peak and gradually unfolds the consequences of that moment, becoming less emotionally intense. Here's the opening line.

> 'Leave?' Audra repeated.

It throws us right in amongst the action. We are clearly meant to understand that, like the other Losers, Bill has just heard from Mike and announced to his wife that he's going back to Derry. Although we're told Audra's repeating herself in astonishment, we didn't actually hear her first statement. We've hit the ground running. Importantly, it's also a moment of friction between characters. Compare this energetic beginning with the end of the section.

> 'And when do I see you again?' she asked softly. He put an arm around her and held her tightly, but he never answered her question.

Uncertainty, silence and lack of resolution. It's as though the energy of the opening has been dissipated. This is entirely appropriate to the role and position of the chapter. Coming after five other accounts of Mike's telephone call – at least two of which start quietly and work up to a funnel-style climax – it would be difficult to see how this sixth section of Chapter 3 could do anything other than cut to the chase. And having thrown us right into the action, a gradual de-escalation is not unexpected.

Pragmatism has to be the most important factor in scene design. Shape the narrative to suit the story's needs at a particular point. But this can (and should) be achieved while taking opportunities to cultivate a distinctive scene profile that appears periodically throughout the novel.

Scene Relationships
Although we're currently analysing the novel as a structure made

up of distinct building blocks, it's important to remember that the building blocks need to connect up with one another to create a continuous storytelling experience. As the lowest level building block, scenes are particularly influenced by their neighbours. The relationship of one scene to the next can be harmonious or discordant in terms of subject matter, tone, length and any number of other factors specific to the particular story. Manipulating these harmonies and discords between scenes is an essential skill if you want to create stories that keep the reader engaged. You're essentially playing with the audience's emotions – at one moment lulling them, then surprising them, or speeding them along then suddenly frustrating them.

Let's first look at an example of discord between scenes. We previously discussed Chapter 17, in which Bev watches the bullies acting crudely at the dump and then witnesses Patrick Hockstetter's death. The scenes that make up the sections of this chapter cover the following material.

- Bev explains to the others how she watched the local bullies lighting their farts at the dump.
- A direct account of the same story.
- A description of the crude home life of one of the bullies.
- The game takes on a sexual character and aggression breaks out.
- One of the bullies revisits a favourite object in the dump - an abandoned refrigerator.
- An account of how the bully murdered his baby brother and kills animals in the refrigerator.
- Flying leeches emerge from the refrigerator and kill the bully. 'It' drags him away.
- Bev is attacked by the flying leeches. She then follows a blood trail to a concrete pipe.
- The Losers are gathered at the refrigerator. They find a message from 'It' written in blood.

You'll notice that, in the course of the chapter, there are various breaks in the continuity of action. There are hindsight episodes (which have a different viewpoint and location as well as a different timeframe) and episodes that leap forward in time (to allow all the

Losers to get to the refrigerator after hearing Bev's story). Nevertheless, the chapter remains a distinct unit that drives the main story forward by a single, clear step. Namely, we find out where the entrance to the creature's lair is thanks to Patrick Hockstetter's death. The various digressions along the way create a sense of cragginess and richness, but Stephen King never allows us to spend too long straying from the path in case we lose our sense of direction.

As we saw in the discussion of sections, a reasonably common feature of scene design in *IT* is the use of brief digressions into a mini-scene. This similarly has the effect of breaking up the texture of the storytelling as it involves a shift in time and/or viewpoint. The effect is usually one of thematic deepening and contextualising of the action in the containing scene. For example, in Chapter 10, section 3, at the reunion dinner, Ben tells the other Losers the story of how he came to lose weight. We never leave dialogue format, but Ben's individual speeches are quite long and immersive, punctuated only by occasional references to his gestures or surroundings. This mini-scene serves to underline the meaning of the reunion. It reveals some of the personal suffering that still needs to be resolved by members of the group, but also illustrates the intimacy that still exists between them after 27 years.

Another important technique that involves discord between neighbouring scenes is not apparent in the Chapter 17 example above. However, it will already be familiar to you. It's the good old cliffhanger – a moment of high tension that only gets resolved after some interval or break in the story. As we all know, it's a very effective way of keeping an audience engaged. For example, section 9 of Chapter 19 ends in the middle of an attack on Eddie by Henry Bowers (as an adult). It's a moment of extreme drama, but section 10 lets it drop and instead talks about Richie, Stan and Eddie as kids, discussing religion and responding to the news that Henry (as a kid) has gone crazy. It's not until section 11 that we see the outcome of the fight. Eddie kills Henry. This is another good example of how a fractured, discordant progression between scenes can sometimes create more richness and interest for the reader.

Now let's consider an example of a harmonious relationship between scenes. In Chapter 4, the transition between the scene that ends section 9 and the scene that starts section 10 is a good example. The section 9 scene describes how Ben escapes from the bullies by creeping through the undergrowth of the Barrens. He can hear the voices of the bullies somewhere nearby. When the section 10 scene takes over, we find Ben still hiding amongst the undergrowth of the Barrens. But rather than hearing the voices of his pursuers, he hears the voices of some other kids playing. This will lead into the main substance of the scene: meeting the other Losers and planning the dam building. The author has focused in on one particular sense at the moment of transition, but cleverly changed the emotions associated with it. This creates a feeling of flow while allowing for a distinctly new dramatic direction.

Scenes don't just create harmony or discord with those that come immediately before and after them. They are sometimes used as part of a scene sequence that together creates a single dramatic moment. For example, the scenes that come just before some climactic episode often help to prepare the reader for the big event. Section 6 of Chapter 21 is just such a moment of extreme drama. It's at the point in the story when the kids fight their way past terrifying apparitions to reach the inner sanctum of 'It'. In acknowledgement of this dramatic importance, the scene spreads out over 17 pages. By contrast, sections 4 and 5, which lead up to that dramatic encounter, are much shorter – just 3 pages and 1 page respectively. Both describe the finding of bodies from the 1950s – ominous events that suggest the creature is near at hand. The sense of anticipation is increased by the brevity of the two scenes concerned. You could say they have a rhythm like a thumping heartbeat or heavy breathing.

Short scenes are also used to bring us down from a dramatic climax. In section 6 of Chapter 16, we see the decisive confrontation between Eddie and his controlling mother. It ends with his mother withdrawing in distress and represents a major turning point in Eddie's psychological struggle. As a result, it's given a generous 14 pages. The section that follows it, which simply describes Eddie's emotional state after the encounter, is just 1 page long. It's a way of quickly and tidily handling the fallout from the major event that just happened, drawing out the consequences while lowering the emotional temperature.

Narrative Threads

As promised, we now change our critical approach. We're going to start considering *IT* as a collection of strands that extend through the text in parallel. The key strands that I'll be concerned with are the novel's story spine and subplots.

Story Spine

Much has been written about the idea of the story spine. But, in my view, it's quite a simple concept. It's the plot strand without which the novel could not happen. It should initiate the story, it should set in motion the central conflict of the story, it should play a role in the resolution of that conflict and, along the way, it should motivate a significant number of major plot turning points. As you can imagine, a novel would be flabby and directionless without one.

So, applying this definition, which story strand has the strongest claim to be the spine of *IT*. Below, I've provided a list of what I consider the novel's main plot strands.

- Bill and the death of Georgie
- The promise to return to Derry
- Romantic interest in Bev
- Henry Bowers and the other bullies
- Richie's cold family life
- Stan's religious shame
- Bev and her father
- Tom and Bev
- Audra and Bill
- Eddie and his mother

In my view, it's the strand relating to Bill and the death of Georgie that should be considered the spine of the novel. All the features of my working definition seem to apply to it. Most obviously, it's the substance of the very first chapter. It's also closely associated with the novel's main conflict. That is to say, when Georgie is killed in Chapter 1, shortly followed by Adrian Mellon in Chapter 2, we understand that the struggle with 'It' will be the conflict at the heart of the novel. At the other end of the novel, the Bill and Georgie plot strand is a prominent feature of the resolution of the struggle against 'It'. Most obviously, the creature adopts the form of Bill's little brother to try to protect its inner sanctum from the Losers

(Chapter 21). But also, the defeat of 'It' is immediately followed by an encounter between Bill and a carefree boy with a paper boat (previously seen skateboarding) who looks just like Georgie (Chapter 23, section 8). It's a brief but important scene that confirms the full resolution of Bill's guilt over Georgie's death – albeit with a nagging sense that the whole horrific cycle of death and guilt could be about to repeat itself with a new boy, a new flood and a new paper sailing boat. In the central parts of the novel, the Bill and Georgie strand displays another aspect of the typical story spine structure: it repeatedly motivates key plot turning points. For example, during the dam building Bill's account of a photograph album that acts as a portal for Pennywise motivates the kids' exchange of supernatural experiences – a key episode that galvanises the resistance to 'It' (Chapter 7). In another turning point, later on, Bill's takes Richie to Georgie's bedroom, shows him the photograph album and persuades him to believe in the supernatural (Chapter 8). Later still, it's the desire to take revenge on Georgie's killer that drives Bill to lead the attacks at Neibolt Street (Chapter 8 and Chapter 18). These are moments when the balance of power shifts in the conflict with 'It'.

Subplots

The remaining strands in the list above have the status of subplots. In other words, they don't set the novel in motion, the story could plausibly have happened without them, they don't initiate or resolve the novel's main conflict and they motivate plot points that are relatively minor. Essentially, they're dependent on the actual story spine, like climbing plants growing up a tree. For example, consider the plot strand that relates to romantic interest in Bev. Like all the other subplots, it's introduced in the first half of the novel, but not in the first couple of chapters. It's also not associated with the initiation of the conflict with 'It'. Moreover, when you consider the plot points that are associated with the romantic/sexual plot strand, you don't feel that their dramatic importance is at all comparable to that of the story spine. Here's a list of those plot points.

- Ben can barely speak to Bev to wish her a good summer
- Ben gives Bev a Haiku on a postcard from the library

- Richie charts with Bev on a bench
- Richie and Ben accompany Bev to the movies
- Ben fantasises about protecting her from her father
- Bev experiences romantic feelings for Bill
- Bev's clothing is torn open during the struggle with the werewolf
- Grown-up Bev and Bill have sex
- As youngsters, the Losers engage in an act of sexual bonding
- Grown-up Bev and Ben plan to be with one another, but eventually she forgets that Tom was abusive and decides to go and search for him (she has even forgotten that he's dead)

The story of *IT* – the story of a struggle with supernatural evil – could happily proceed without any of those episodes. It's true that the author chose to include a sexual bonding episode in the aftermath of one very important plot point – the 1958 defeat of 'It' in Chapter 22, section 12 – but the sexual content is certainly not essential to that plot point. It's a strange moment that generates strong opinions. The controversy is partly down to the uncomfortable nature of the content, but also, I believe, partly down to the marginal nature of the romantic/sexual plot strand – it just doesn't seem important enough to have a scene close to the climax of the novel's central conflict.

So, romantic/sexual interest in Bev is clearly a subplot in terms of narrative significance. But that doesn't make it unnecessary or frivolous. Subplots are in no way pointless distractions. What they do, principally, is enrich the texture of a novel. The plot points listed above fulfil that role in several ways. Firstly, they contribute to those layers of meaning that I described above in the chapter about theme, creating a more profound reading experience. *IT* is typical in the way it achieves this. It does it by intersecting subplots with the story spine and with one another at key moments. For example, when Ben is attacked by bullies in Chapter 4, section 9, he's thinking about how much he likes Bev, but also recalling his dreams of 'It'.

> Ben's pleasant fantasy of Beverly was suddenly broken by one far more grim: what if a dead hand flopped out of that culvert right now, right this second, while he was looking? And suppose that

when he turned to find a phone and call the police, a clown was standing there? A funny clown wearing a baggy suit with big orange puffs for buttons? Suppose –

A hand fell on Ben's shoulder, and he screamed.

There was laughter. He whirled around, shrinking against the white fence separating the safe, sane sidewalk of Kansas Street from the wildly undisciplined Barrens (the railing creaked audibly), and saw Henry Bowers …

This one episode pulls together the romantic interest subplot, the bullying subplot and the story-spine struggle with 'It'. The collision between them brings a new dimension to the psychological theme layer of the novel. In a few off-hand sentences, it suggests that Ben's social awkwardness and his suffering at the hands of Henry Bowers are very similar phenomena – as though he has a taunting bully in his own head telling him he's too fat to be loveable. It also suggests that 'It' can metaphorically represent both forms of suffering.

To take another example, Ben is once again daydreaming about Bev in Chapter 18, section 4. Specifically, he's fantasising about the idea of saving her from her father.

Kill him? Hanscom says, the Gary Cooper smile still lingering on his lips. No way, baby. He may be a creep, but he's still your father. I might have roughed him up a little, but that's only because when someone talks wrong to you I get a little hot under the collar. You know?

She throws her arms around him and kisses him (on the lips! on the LIPS!). I love you, Ben! she sobs. He can feel her small breasts pressing firmly against his chest and –

This takes place as the kids are waiting for their silver slugs to cool and harden, providing them with ammunition that will work against 'It'. This time, the intersection of subplot and story spine is enriching the social theme layer of the novel as well as exploring psychological territory. It suggests that 'It' represents the cruelty or indifference to children that's endemic in Derry, and which Bev's abusive father is just one example of.

In addition to this thematic layering role, subplots generally enlarge on a novel's characterisations and relationships. This is how we come to know and like all the main characters – each is involved in one or more subplots that put them under the spotlight. Bev, for example, not only figures in the romantic interest subplot but also in the subplot relating to her husband Tom (who spots her as a vulnerable target, treats her in a controlling and violent way and then pursues her when she travels to Derry) and the subplot relating to her father (who emotionally, physically and sexually abuses her). While this tangled nexus of subplots is building up layers of psychological and social meaning, it is also imparting quite a lot of diverse personal information about Bev. That, in itself, has a value to readers hungry for emotional connection. As a kid, Bev was obedient, respectful and hardworking – also something of a tomboy. As an adult, she's emotionally vulnerable but capable of showing grit. She is a secret smoker. She works as a fashion designer and developed her own clothes label. She has a friend called Kay. She has red hair and long legs. And so it goes on. We can't help but root for someone who is known to us in such a multi-dimensional way.

A further function of subplots is to create tension. Tension is always fascinating to readers, no matter how minor. It's easy to see where this tension comes from in the romantic interest subplot. Bill, Ben and Richie are all interested in Bev to some degree. Although it's rarely spoken about, we feel the potential for conflict. On one of the occasions when the tension does surface, it's evoked in the most minimal terms. Ben notices a special electricity between Bill and Bev after the encounter with the werewolf.

> 'Thank you, Bill,' she said, and for one hot, smoking moment their eyes locked directly. Bill did not look away this time. His gaze was firm, adult.
> 'W-W-W-Welcome,' he said.
> Good luck, Big Bill, Ben thought, and he turned away from that gaze. It was hurting him, hurting him in a deeper place than any Vampire or Werewolf would ever be able to reach. But all the same, there was such a thing as propriety. The word he didn't know; on the concept he was very clear. Looking at them when they were looking at each other that way would be as wrong as looking at her breasts when she let go of the front of her blouse to pull Bill's t-shirt over her head. If that's the way it is. But you'll never love her the way I do. Never.

There may only be a few sentences describing Ben's moment of jealousy, but it feels much larger than that. It's given great emotional power by the fact that a potential conflict situation has been allowed to develop over the course of the novel without anyone speaking about it or releasing it in any other way.

As I mentioned at the start of this section, *IT* has up to ten different subplots. All have a significant (though not indispensable) role in the novel, contributing to layers of theme, characterisation and tension. I can only imagine that coordinating them as they intersected with one another and the story spine must have been a major challenge for Stephen King. However, it's probably true to say that the sheer length of *IT* eased this problem somewhat. The amount of narrative space available in a novel of more than 1000 pages must give an author more freedom to introduce plot strands and develop pretexts for intersecting them. It follows, therefore, that a shorter novel would almost certainly have fewer subplots if the author wanted to achieve approximately the same level of plot 'density' that we see in *IT*.

Takeaway

- Structural analysis can consider a text's subdivisions but also the strands that run through it.
  - Building blocks
    - Parts
      - Consider using a five-act structure like that described by Freytag.
      - Distinguish each act with a title-page quotation.
      - Make sure that each of the acts contains chapters that share distinctive qualities.
    - Chapters
      - Provide titles that describe the essentials of the chapter but leave surprises.
      - Some chapters should be devoted to one character's affairs and viewpoint.
      - Group-centred chapters can pass the viewpoint around.
      - Interludes can be used to refresh the reader and increase stakes.

- Interludes may be linked to the main narrative by shared imagery.
- If an epilogue is set some time after the end of the main narrative it is better able to deepen thematic meaning.
- Sections
  - Use sections to enable longer chapter structures.
  - One scene per section is common in *IT*, but many other arrangements occur.
- Scenes
  - A scene is a piece of continuous action with the same set of characters in the same location, revolving around a single conflict or motivation that's resolved either satisfactorily or unsatisfactorily by the end.
  - One characteristic scene type in *IT* begins with generalities and funnels us into a moment of intense action.
  - Also consider emulating the novel's other scene types, including those that throw us into the midst of the action.
- Scene relationships
  - Relationships between adjacent scenes can be harmonious or discordant.
  - Sequences of scenes can together create a single dramatic moment.
- Narrative threads
  - Story spine
    - A story spine is the plot strand without which the novel could not happen. It should initiate the story, it should set in motion the central conflict of the story, it should play a

150

role in the resolution of that conflict and, along the way, it should motivate a significant number of major plot turning points.

- The story of Bill's guilt over the death of Georgie is the spine of *IT*.

- Subplots
  - Subplots are inessential to the main plot of the novel.
  - Subplots do generate thematic meaning at points where they intersect with one another and with the story spine.
  - Subplots also enlarge on characterisation.
  - A subplot is an ideal setting for creating tension between characters.

6. BUILDING INTENSITY

'... a Spider from beyond the fevered imaginings of whatever inmates
may live in the deepest depths of hell.'
– Stephen King, *IT*

An essential requirement for action-based popular fiction,
including horror fiction, is to gradually ratchet up the intensity level
over time. In the 'Toolkit for Terror' chapter above, we saw an
intensification technique that's specific to horror – the frequency of
supernatural occurrences increases markedly over the course of the
novel. In this chapter, I'd like to discuss some of the other ways in
which the reader's experience of *IT* becomes more profound,
gripping and satisfying as the story progresses.

Stakes

The term 'stakes' is often misunderstood. Many people use it
casually, meaning something like 'danger'. But stakes are actually
associated with a very specific form of danger – it's the risk that
characters knowingly embrace in order to achieve their goals. If a
character is persecuted through no fault of their own, we might feel
sorry for them, but we won't feel excited about their actions. In
fact, we're more likely to feel depressed on their behalf, which is
not the frame of mind an author should put their readers in.
Similarly, if a character suddenly decides to play Russian roulette
for no very good reason, we may feel a certain amount of morbid
curiosity about the outcome, but there's never going to be a sense

of excitement. In fact, we'll probably consider it rather silly. That would be true no matter how well we know the character. By contrast, when a character has a particular goal, understands the risks associated with it and goes ahead anyway, there's a thrill associated with watching events play out. The thrill is usually derived from the bravery of the character's decision, but it could equally be derived from the pitiable nature of the decision if we feel that it's primarily a self-sacrificial gesture. Both of those emotional responses to heightened stakes are seen in *IT*.

The sense of bravery around the Losers' decision to come together and launch an attack on 'It' – both in 1958 and 1985 – is clear. They don't have to come. They could continue with their damaged but functional lives. But they choose to reach for the light instead. In the latter part of the novel, the risks associated with that course of action become ever greater and ever clearer to the Losers. From Chapter 12 onwards, they're not just facing contained threats, they're facing murderous individuals set on doing them personal harm. Up to that point, two characters had been the victims of deadly attacks (Georgie and Adrian Mellon) but they weren't members of the Losers' Club and hadn't chosen to confront 'It'. Furthermore, the non-deadly encounters with 'It' that occurred prior to Chapter 12 were always constrained in some way. For example, 'It' was hidden within a photo album, a fortune cookie, a plughole, a bully who is violent but still just a school boy, and so on. These are locations and situations that could easily be avoided by the Losers. But in Chapter 12, the risks associated with confronting 'It' become much more personal and potentially deadly for the Losers. It's at this point that Henry and Tom are mobilised against them.

And the stakes continue to rise. In Chapter 16, section 3, for example, the bullies who have been persecuting the kids in 1958 definitively cease being just unruly children and become terrifying adult psychopaths. That's the point at which Henry Bowers faces down an adult who is in a position to discipline him.

Once the Losers hit the tunnels in Part 5 of the novel, all the forces that 'It' can muster are brought to bear on them, both in 1958 and 1985. The words of 'It' confirm that this is the result of the Losers' free decision go on the attack against the creature.

It would kill the children because they had, by some amazing accident, hurt It.

Freely accepted risk like this is the essence of high stakes.

I mentioned above that our thrill response to high stakes can sometimes involve a sense of the piteousness of the heroes' actions rather than a sense of their bravery. This occurs in the latter part of *IT* too. In Chapter 22, section 5, the adult Bill finds himself on the edge of the deadlights, about to be drawn in, but suddenly Eddie steps up and helps him to escape. The result is that Eddie dies having lost an arm, just like Georgie. I'm tempted to quote the famous biblical passage 'Greater love hath no man than this, that a man lay down his life for his friends,' because there's definitely a Christ-like self-sacrificial nobility about Eddie's actions. He sees the risk and embraces it anyway.

Twists

One of the key techniques for raising the stakes in a novel is the good old plot twist. When an unexpected danger occurs, it encourages the reader to think that the heroes might have bitten off more than they can chew. Accordingly, there are more and more such moments towards the end of *IT*. Unlike standard plot developments, these are moments when it becomes clear that the author has systematically misled you about the course of the action. For example, in Chapter 20, section 1, we are first given the impression that Tom is going to take revenge on Bev and Bill.

> She had used a belt on his (kicked me in the) balls and run off and she now had cheated on him … she was going to get the whuppin of all whuppins – first her and then Denbrough …

However, it transpires in section 2 that he is actually going to go after Bill's wife, Audra. The moment when this is revealed is a masterful demonstration of how to create a shocking plot twist. Audra has had an unpleasant encounter with 'It' via her dreams and the TV set. She's in the process of dealing with that when a hand suddenly grabs her.

> 'Haven't I seen you in the movies?' Tom Rogan whispered.

The unexpected interjection of Tom into a section concerned with

WRITE LIKE STEPHEN KING

other things is a big part of the shock effect, and the fact that this happens at the end of the section is an amplifying factor since it adds a cliffhanger element to the twist. The details of Tom's appearance are also superbly sinister. The whispered nicety has a concealed sense of malice that's so much more terrifying than an outright threat.

Other twists in the latter part of the novel include the following.

1. Henry surviving potentially fatal injuries inflicted by Mike and going on to attack Eddie. An enemy coming back to life unexpectedly is a very common twist type.
2. The death of Eddie. Up to that point he had been sitting on the sidelines as Bill and Richie dealt with 'It'.
3. 'It' becoming the viewpoint character. We had become accustomed to the idea that this monster was a totally incomprehensible evil.
4. The act of sexual union between Bev and each of the other Losers in the 1958 narrative. We have been trained to expect that just one hero will 'get the girl'. Some twists play with our expectations of literary convention.
5. After the 1985 defeat of 'It', it becomes clear that the Losers are once again succumbing to forgetfulness. Literary convention dictates that heroes learn from their adventures rather than lapsing back into old errors.

Emotions

One of the most obvious ways in which the novel intensifies over time is a rise in its emotional pitch. The characters experience and express more powerful emotions in the later chapters.

It's hard to imagine the following description of a character's inner experience occurring at any point other than the climactic action in Chapter 22, section 3.

> He felt his own fury, clean and singing, as his eyes fixed on Its eyes.

Elsewhere in the novel, we've heard Bill voicing his rage against 'It' – for example, when he attacked the creature at Neibolt Street.

> Ben heard Bill bellow: 'You k-k-killed my brother, you fuh-fuh-fucking BITCH!'

But on that earlier occasion there was a sense of shrillness about Bill's words, betraying impotence. By comparison, the emotion expressed in Chapter 23 is cold, hard and absolute.

In the aftermath of the confrontation with 'It', we see the same reaching for emotional transcendence and purity in a positive vein. Consider the passage in the Epilogue that describes Bill's bike ride with Audra – in particular, this sentence.

> 'Hi-yo Silver, AWAYYYYYYY!' Bill Denbrough cried deliriously, and rushed down the hill toward whatever there would be, aware for one last time of Derry as his place, aware most of all that he was alive under a real sky, and that all was desire, desire, desire.

There's an ecstatic quality here that even exceeds descriptions of Bill as a child riding his bike. On each of the earlier occasions when Bill used the phrase 'Hi-yo Silver' to begin a journey, the author applied one of the following verbs: 'shouted', 'screamed', 'bellowed' and 'yelled'. There's a boyish roughness to those words that's almost funny. By comparison, 'cried deliriously' expresses a feeling of transcendence that is almost religious. The same effect is created by the repetition of 'desire, desire, desire'.

Transcendence

It's not just the emotional landscape of *IT* that's pushed to a higher pitch. Other aspects of the novel's action are similarly taken to extreme levels in the concluding chapters.

The manifestations of 'It' undergo a particularly noticeable change. In the first half of the novel, we begin with the clown persona, Pennywise, but move on to something that's less easily pinned down. At Neibolt Street, in Chapter 8, Richie sees the creature as a werewolf, but to Bill it's still the clown. Then, in Chapter 15, two of the Losers have a vision of 'It' arriving from somewhere beyond the earth. And there's an even more extreme manifestation when we arrive at the climactic action. The creature's spider guise is just a dramatic convenience, because the real appearance of the creature is so pure in its extremity that you can't see it without dying – as Tom finds out in Chapter 21, section 3.

We see a similar push for transcendence in relation to the setting of the novel's final action. The deadlights – where 'It' lives – is a dimension so far removed from our own world that it can't be encompassed by the human mind. In describing it, Stephen King resorts to a series of vague and suggestive images.

> And beyond him, coming up fast, Richie could see/sense something that finally dried up his laughter. It was a barrier, something of a strange, non-geometrical shape that his mind could not grasp. Instead his mind translated it as best it could, as it had translated the shape of It into a Spider, allowing Richie to think of it as a colossal gray wall made of fossilized wooden stakes. These stakes went forever up and forever down, like the bars of a cage. And from between them shone a great blind light. It glared and moved, smiled and snarled. The light was alive.

Not all novels are able to push their setting to such an absolute level, but it's normal for climactic action to take place in an arena that's special in some way. For example, it could be prestigious, inaccessible or simply very dangerous. If a horror story or thriller is set in a skyscraper, the final climax is going to take place on the roof or a window-cleaner's cradle hanging down the side, not in the canteen.

Going Deeper

As we've seen, there is a huge array of techniques used by Stephen King to convey the themes of *IT*. Some are quite obvious. Into that category I would place the personal stories of each of the Losers. Their biographies, characterised by a chronic inability to avoid harmful behaviour, are a clear illustration of the theme of repetition. Some means of conveying thematic meaning are much more subtle than that – for example, the use of repeating patterns within the text. But, as the novel proceeds, there is a tendency to state thematic ideas more openly and clearly. For example, the title of Chapter 20 is 'The Circle Closes'. You couldn't imagine a more explicit statement of the idea circularity and repetition. It tells us outright that we can expect to see a cycle of repeated suffering concluded during that chapter.

There's another particularly striking way in which thematic material is openly stated in the latter part of the novel. As the main characters approach the end of their stories, they attain new depths of insight into the psychological, social and metaphysical issues underlying their struggle with 'It'. Armed with this new self-understanding, they begin interpreting their own circumstances.

You could almost say they become authors of their own fate. This trend begins in Chapter 16, section 8. Eddie is lying in a hospital bed with the other Losers gathered around him. He reflects on the significance of his earlier argument with his mother.

> We're passing over, Eddie thought. Passing over into something new – we're on the border. But what's on the other side? Where are we going? Where?

It's a barely formed thought, but it grasps at an essential truth – he and all the other Losers have, up until now, been ensnared by forces holding them back in old versions of themselves. For him, it was the clinginess of his mother. Each of the other kids is oppressed by a similarly limiting influence. But now there's a hope of redemption. Eddie has proven to himself that those oppressive forces can be overcome and that something better (as yet unknown) can replace them. In effect, the thought quoted above is another clear statement of the theme of repetition. It acknowledges that the past was all about harmful cycles of behaviour and looks forward to personal redemption.

In Chapter 19, we see an even more striking example of characters openly stating thematic meaning. In section 5 of that chapter, we find Bev lying in bed after having sex with Bill. Looking back over the events of 1958 and looking forward to the events that will inevitably happen in the tunnels on the following day, she reflects on the repetitious nature of their relationship and of their struggle with 'It'.

> Her happiness here with him, after all these years, was real. She knew that because of its bitter undertaste. There was tonight, and perhaps there would be another time for them tomorrow morning. Then they would go down in the sewers as they had before, and they would find their It. The circle would close even tighter and their present lives would merge smoothly with their own childhoods; they would become like creatures on some crazy Moebius strip.

A literary critic couldn't summarise better the psychological and metaphysical issues that underlie the stories of these two characters. It's a far cry from her state of mind at the start of the novel. Back then, she was unable to fully grasp her own troubled condition. You'll recall that, in Chapter 9, section 1 she visited her friend Kay after being beaten by Tom but couldn't seem to take in the other woman's advice on how to break the harmful cycle of bad relationships.

> 'He didn't use his belt on me,' Bev said. The lie was automatic ... and so was the deep shame which brought a miserable flush to her cheeks. 'If you're done with Tom, you ought to be done with the lies as well,' Kay said ...

In the ten chapters that separate those two episodes, Bev undergoes a dramatic personal journey, deep into the truth of her own condition.

Subplot Intersection

As we have previously seen, a major function of subplots is to enrich the texture of a novel. One way in which they do this is by adding layers of meaning to the story – psychological and social insights especially. In my view, this thematic layering is most profound and productive in *IT* at moments when subplots intersect with the story spine or with one another. Throughout the novel, there are moments when a sudden collision between different plot strands creates a flash of insight. Most often, this relates to psychological issues affecting characters or social structures that characterise Derry as a whole. You could think of them as mini volcanoes, and the subplots as tectonic plates that move against one another causing eruptions of fresh thematic truth where they meet. This body of truth builds up into a crust that's thickest near the volcano but spreads out over the whole fictional landscape, affecting how we interpret the details of the novel.

Earlier, I discussed a pair of examples involving Ben. We twice find him thinking about his beloved Bev at moments when an encounter with 'It' and/or the local bullies is about to take place. This collision between the romantic subplot, the bullying subplot and the central struggle with 'It' is highly significant. It suggests that Ben's shyness and comfort eating are closely related to the social evil of bullying. Both are harmful behaviours that repeat themselves over and over and consequently prevent a person from flourishing. Moreover, both can be represented by the metaphor of supernatural oppression.

Without doubt, these intersections and flashes of insight

become more frequent in the later chapters of *IT*. It's a complicated picture to paint, but here are some of the complex plot-strand pile-ups that take place in the later chapters.

- Bullying subplot meets story spine: The main subject of the bullying subplot, Henry Bowers, is co-opted by 'It' and used to mount a counterattack on the Losers. During his fight with Eddie in the hotel, Henry incoherently shouts about the rock fight that the two of them engaged in as kids. It's an insight into the sheer pettiness of evil. His mind has been going round and round in circles of grievance for 27 years.

- Mike/racism subplot meets story spine: Henry's assault on Mike, in which he repeatedly screams the word 'nigger', powerfully suggests that racism is another cyclical affliction of society.

- Bev and Tom subplot meets story spine: Bev's persecutor Tom is co-opted in the same way as Henry, adding domestic abuse to the novel's catalogue of perennial evils that all seem to draw on a single principle – the thing that 'It' represents.

- Bev and Tom subplot meets Bill and Audra subplot meets story spine: Tom chooses to get at Bill by attacking his wife Audra. This intersection suggests that a primitive sexual drive is one of the energies that evil draws on.

- Bullying subplot meets story spine: In the tunnels under Derry in 1985, the bodies of several of the local bullies from 1958 are found. It is pointed out that their bodies remain childlike. This suggests that becoming locked into harmful, repetitive behaviours like bullying is a form of death.

- Bill and Audra subplot meets story spine: Audra is trapped in a web and placed in a coma by 'It'. She doesn't emerge from her unresponsive state until Bill recognises that she needs the same dangerous freedom that he experiences when riding his childhood bike. It seems there is a possibility of redemption from the death-like state of clinging to old versions of yourself.

These are just some of the more obvious plot intersections from the latter part of the novel. As you can see, they create a rich texture that's quite different from the earlier parts of the novel. In the opening chapters, the author takes time to clearly establish each individual subplot and allows them to develop in relative isolation.

This increasing density of thematic meaning is an extremely important aspect of the novel's gradually rising intensity. All the greatest novels – both popular and literary – leave one with a feeling of understanding the world a little better, and I believe Stephen King achieves that in *IT,* largely thanks to the eruptions of insight that take place when plot strands collide.

Recommitment

At key moments in the novel, the author takes the opportunity to clear the decks of all distractions and have the Losers unambiguously state their commitment to the central conflict of the plot – the struggle to overcome 'It'. One of these moments occurs in Chapter 10, section 5, at the end of the reunion dinner. Bill takes a vote on whether to press home the attack that they've begun by returning to Derry.

> 'All right; I g-guess the question is, do we stay and fight or do we forget the whole thing? Those in favor of staying?' No one at the table moved at all for perhaps five seconds ...

All present eventually raise their hands. They are now locked into a specific task and their desire to succeed in it is clear. This naturally rallies the reader's enthusiasm too.

A similar episode occurs in Chapter 20, section 4, after Henry's attack on Eddie at the hotel. Bill crystallises their options and forces the others to commit one way or another.

> 'D-Do you still w-w-want to g-g-go to the p-p-police, Bev?'
> ...
> She looked at the four of them. 'We swore it,' she said. 'We swore. Bill's brother ... Stan ... all the others ... and now Mike. I'm ready, Bill.'
> Bill looked at the others.
> Richie nodded. 'Okay, Big Bill. Let's try.'
> Ben said, 'The odds look worse than ever. We're two short now.'
> Bill said nothing.
> 'Okay.' Ben nodded. 'She's right. We swore.'
> 'E-E-Eddie?'
> Eddie smiled wanly. 'I guess I get another pigger-back down that ladder, huh? If the ladder's still there.'

Having renewed their commitment, there's only one place they can go next – the tunnels under Derry.

It's not surprising that these moments of clear decision-making occur at natural pivot points in the story structure. The first is midway through the novel – commonly a point at which major plot turns take place. The second is 88% of the way through the novel, when the reader is beginning to sense that the final action has to happen now or never.

Completeness

When a novel's story concludes, what the author wants is for the reader to go away feeling that everything is complete. Some of this is just about tidying up loose ends. But I don't mean that in a flippant way. Certain loose ends can be extremely important and absolutely must be fully resolved. In particular, it's crucial to ensure that the novel's big evil is comprehensively defeated – unless, of course the novel is part of a series. In Chapter 22, section 9 of *IT*, for example, Stephen King has the Losers crush the spider's offspring. It signals that there is absolutely no coming back for the creature.

But there is a deeper form of completion that readers crave. It can be described as poetic justice. That term refers to the sense of 'rightness' or 'appropriateness' that we get when a character's story takes a course that seems to be exactly what they need or deserve. Often, it relates to the fate suffered by a villain. In such cases, the means of the villain's downfall will typically recall some feature of their villainy. But poetic justice can also be applied to the hero of a story. In these cases, the character's story will end with an experience that completes their personal journey in some way.

The moment in Chapter 21, section 9, when 'It' appears in the form of Georgie is a good example of poetic justice for a hero.

> It was George wavering up the tunnel toward him, George, still dressed in his blood-spattered yellow rainslicker. One sleeve dangled limp and useless. George's face was white as cheese and his eyes were shiny silver. They fixed on Bill's own. 'My boat!' Georgie's lost voice rose, wavering, in the tunnel. 'I can't find it, Bill, I've looked everywhere and I can't find it and now I'm dead and it's your fault your fault YOUR FAULT –'

The final words of that passage lay bare the deepest wound in Bill's character and present him with a means of healing it. To find redemption, he must confront and overcome the specific evil that he fell victim to at the start of the novel – guilt over the death of his brother. Of course, 'It' is both the cause of that guilt (having killed Georgie) and a metaphor for insidious, soul-destroying guilt feelings. Destroying the creature is therefore 'right' on both a literal and a metaphorical level. This is a very typical pattern of poetic justice for heroes: defeat, struggle, revisit the circumstances of defeat, redeem yourself through victory.

Importantly, the harmful effects of Bill's early experience have been clearly signalled to us throughout the novel. As a child, he can't help but visit Georgie's bedroom. There, he discovers a photo album that allows 'It' to enter his world. Later, he mounts an attack on 'It' at Neibolt Street. In the course of the fight, he screams out his rage over the death of Georgie. And the pain doesn't end with the 1958 defeat of 'It'. As an adult, Bill endlessly recycles his childhood trauma by writing horror novels. He also shares his guilt feelings with Bev when they become intimate once again. Without all this build-up, and without the clear statement 'it's your fault your fault YOUR FAULT –' the moment when Georgie comes shuffling down the tunnel would have fallen flat. As it is, we feel a powerful sense of rightness.

As I've previously argued, Bill's struggle with guilt is the principle motivation behind the novel's story spine. Without it, the group wouldn't have been drawn together by Bill in 1958 and the struggle with 'It' wouldn't have ensued. Because of this close association with the story spine, a moment of poetic justice that satisfactorily rounds off Bill's story (for the moment) is a great way of concluding the main action of the novel as a whole.

Not all novel plots have such an intimate connection between the hero's character and the story spine. If there isn't such a connection, there's still room for poetic justice. The hero's story can still begin with a personal trauma and conclude with a scene that recalls it. It's just that the emotional pay-off will be less. Poetic justice can also find its way into such novels in the form of an appropriate comeuppance for the villain, as I mentioned earlier. However, in my opinion, the most effective stories do make the story spine personal to the hero in some way. And in such cases, it almost seems wasteful not to have a scene late in the story that maximises poetic justice for the hero.

Release

Having wound the reader up with suspense, concern, insight and other powerful emotions over the course of a novel, it's important to provide a release after the climax. Stephen King does that in Chapter 22, section 6. It takes the form of a series of energetic and funny micro-narratives about the apocalyptic aftermath of the Losers' attack on 'It' in 1985. The effect is like a firework display rewarding the reader for staying to the end of the party. Here's one of the anecdotes. It relates to the fate of a doctor in Derry.

> His exit-line from the world, spoken back over his shoulder as he went through the front door, pulling his hat firmly down to his ears, was: 'Don't be so goddamned silly, Hilda. This is nothing but a capful of rain. You should have seen it in '57! That was a storm!' As Dr Hale turned back onto West Broadway, a manhole cover in front of the Mueller place suddenly lifted off like the payload of a Redstone rocket. It decapitated the good doctor so quickly and neatly that he walked on another three steps before collapsing, dead, on the sidewalk.

As you can see, it has a dark humour to it, as well as a brevity and vividness of imagination that's energising for the reader. Similar stories come one after another, rapid-fire style, almost like a stand-up routine.

It's important to note that Chapter 22, section 6, is not the climax of the novel, it's a stage after the successful 1958 and 1985 attacks on 'It'. So, it's actually part of the declining action. While the anecdote quoted above is tangentially related to the wider events of the novel – via the reference to the 1957 storm when Georgie died – it doesn't add anything to the novel's main narrative other than a sense of release. That's because the climactic action has largely completed and capped off the main story.

NOT Pace

A final, slightly unexpected note about the latter stages of *IT*: the novel is quite unusual among action-based genre novels in that its action doesn't noticeably pick up pace towards the climax.

In action-based novels, you often see the illusion of pace being created by reporting more events more scantily in the space of a single scene or chapter. Perhaps surprisingly, the use of shorter scenes or chapters is not an important contributing factor in the illusion of pace. Although, short sections are used in the latter parts of *IT* to create a sense of heightened anticipation (as we saw in the 'Narrative Structure' chapter) this is not really a pacey effect. That's because the sections in question typically report just one or two events each. Read them over again and you'll appreciate just how slow they feel. Section 4 may consist of just 3 pages, but in those 3 pages we only hear about one substantial event (the finding of a body) plus a minor occurrence (wondering which route to take). Section 5 is not that different, devoting its one page to the finding of another body. Even the fact that the same type of event occurs twice in consecutive sections has a slowing effect. The atmosphere at this point just before the climax of the novel is like a fearful anticipation of dreadful events. The opposite of pacey, in fact.

Even those suspenseful scenes that I described in the 'Toolkit for Terror' chapter above eschew the idea of pacey writing. They may progress from a calm opening to a violent manifestation of 'It', but their climax is usually slowed down to a crawl by vivid observations of the terrifying creature. Pace and fear are evidently not always best friends.

Takeaway

- An essential requirement for action-based popular fiction, including horror fiction, is to gradually ratchet up the intensity level over time.
  - o Stakes
    - Stakes are freely chosen risks.
    - The heroes must experience increasing risk linked to a freely chosen conflict.
    - The reader's response to stakes can be excitement or pity for a self-sacrificial act.
  - o Twists
    - Twists raise the stakes, especially if linked to a cliffhanger.
    - They should pile up in the latter part of the novel.

o Emotions
- The climax of the novel should include emotions that are pure in their extremity (positive and negative).

o Transcendence
- Give characters more extreme experiences towards the end of the novel.
- The climax should be in an inaccessible, exclusive or dangerous location.

o Going deeper
- Open and clear expressions of the novel's themes should become more common.

o Subplot intersection
- Intersections between subplots and between subplots and the story spine release thematic meaning.
- These intersections should become more common over the course of the novel.

o Recommitment
- Have the heroes recommit to their task.
- This should occur at natural pivot points in the plot such as the midpoint.

o Completeness
- Readers need to feel completeness at the end of the novel.
- Poetic justice is one factor – a feeling that characters experienced the right outcomes.
- This requires that we know in advance the deepest truths of characters' lives.

o Release
- In the novel's declining action, the emotions can take a playful or celebratory turn.

o NOT pace
- In novels, the illusion of pace is achieved by describing more actions more scantily within a certain space.
- This is not an essential tool for raising the intensity level.

CONCLUSION

Congratulations on reaching the end of the book.

What now?

If you haven't signed up for my email list to get the accompanying exercises, I encourage you to do so. See the special offer at the end of the book for details. Working through those targeted activities is the best way to extract maximum value from this book. They will help you to complete much of the preparation for writing a great horror novel.

I would also encourage you to read the many other novels by Stephen King. As you do so, you'll probably notice quite a few of the structures and stylistic gestures that I've described here. In fact, analysing the similarities and differences will help you internalise the lessons drawn from *IT*.

Not all of what I've pointed out in Stephen King's work will make sense right now ... or maybe ever. But that's OK. It shows you're becoming your own kind of writer. The key is to try lots of techniques and discover what works for you. And I hope, eventually, you will experience a wonderful moment like Bill Denbrough's authorial coming of age:

> ... his head seems to bulge with the story; it is a little scary, the way it needs to get out. He feels that if it cannot escape by way of his racing hand that it will pop his eyes out in its urgency to escape and be concrete. 'Going to knock the shit out of it,' he confides to the blowing winter dark, and laughs a little – a shaky laugh.

APPENDIX 1: PATTERN AND THEME

'Sometimes it comes a little sooner, sometimes a little later ... but it
always comes.'
– Stephen King, *IT*

Earlier, we looked at how building blocks were used in *IT* to create
a long yet compelling story. We also looked at some of the strands
that run through the novel creating a rich reading experience. In
this appendix, I'd like to take a different approach to both those
subjects. It's my opinion that the various structural features of *IT*
(subdivisions, subplots and so on) are used to create distinctive
patterns in the text – rather like the rhythm and rhyme of a poem –
and that these patterns express some of the central themes of the
novel.

Because the themes under discussion are specific to *IT*, this part
of the book may not identify techniques that you can directly
borrow (hence my decision to include it as an appendix), but I
hope it will be a source of inspiration, getting you to think about
novel structure and how you can use it to express your own
themes.

Subdivision Patterns

All the subdivisions in *IT* – scenes, sections, chapters and parts –
are involved in creating patterns that express theme. Here's a
simple example. I previously pointed out that some of the novel's
scenes in turn contain micro-scenes that are briefly allowed to

intrude on the main narrative. Importantly, these small pockets of narrative are often fictional spaces where 'It' can be found lurking. Consider the account of Ben's dream in section 6 of Chapter 4. It's actually a story within a story within a story. He's at the library when he recalls his secure home life – how he would lie comfortably in bed last thing at night. On one such occasion, he dreamed of playing baseball with other kids and hitting a home run. But then Pennywise appears in the dream, blighting his moment of triumph. The nasty creature at the story's core has been revealed and now we return to the main narrative set in the library. In my opinion, occasions like this when the creature turns up in a small narrative pocket are vivid illustrations of a motif that we met earlier. You'll recall that Stephen King not only gives the novel's chief representation of evil in an underground hiding place, but also pulls other examples of subterranean evil into the novel. The prime example is the story of 'The Three Billy Goats Gruff', with its troll under a bridge. This fairy tale keeps reappearing throughout the novel, so it's clearly of great importance to the understanding of the novel. My contention is that the author uses the 'story-within-a-story' structure to create little hidey-holes for his own monster-haunted narrative spaces that the characters and the readers have to pass through.

The theme of subterranean evil is by no means the most important influence on the narrative patterns within *IT*. That honour goes to the theme of repetitious harmful behaviour. In the 'Thematic Layers' chapter, we explored its various expressions. We saw that it has a personal and a social dimension. On the personal side, all the main characters are struggling with psychological, social and supernatural 'demons'. One of the clearest examples is Bev, who keeps repeating unsuitable relationships with men but seizes the opportunity to break the cycle by leaving her husband. This coincides with her decision to go back on the offensive against supernatural evil by returning to Derry. Disappointingly, we hear at the end of the novel that she has left Ben to go and search for Tom, having completely forgotten that he was a domestic tyrant (and even that he's dead). As regards the social expression of repetitious harmful behaviour, we learn from Mike that Derry undergoes a paroxysm of violence every 27 years. Its inhabitants dutifully investigate the outbreaks of child murder but can't acknowledge their own indifference to children's welfare. There is no moment of self-insight for the citizens of Derry in *IT*, and we can only assume that a fresh outbreak of murder will occur in another 27 years if it turns out that 'It' was not properly disposed of in 1985 as in 1958. Basically, everyone in the novel is going round and round in vicious circles, looking for redemption but not quite finding it. Most obviously, the Losers go through an almost identical sequence of actions in 1958 and 1985. They hope to resolve the struggle with 'It' better second time round, and maybe heal the scars of their childhood too, but there is every indication at the end of the novel that they're going to descend into dangerous amnesia, as they did in 1958.

It's clear that the novel's structure has been shaped in order to express this theme of repetition, as well as the accompanying idea of redemption. The most distinctive feature of the novel's narrative is the way two different years run parallel to one another. The author could have chosen to narrate the two stories consecutively. Instead, he alternates between sections devoted to 1957/1958 and sections devoted to 1984/1985. This draws attention to the fact that the stories of the two years are essentially the same – in both, the Losers are oppressed by a supernatural evil they call 'It' and they decide to come together as a group and fight back. It also creates something of a sense of futility around the repetition. Whenever we start to think of the Losers' exploits as a heroic progress towards victory, the novel's structure draws our attention to the fact that they have been here before or will be here again (depending on which year we're talking about). In other words, there is every reason to suspect that repetitious behaviour is inescapable.

However, that cynical take on repetition is not the whole picture. There's more to the two-year structure of *IT* than that. In the course of the novel, we find the two years mingling more and more closely and finally almost completely merging. This process is broken into several stages, which are clearly defined by the novel's subdivisions. At the start of the novel, in Part 1, chapters are dedicated to specific years – 1957, then 1984 and finally 1985, as indicated by the chapter titles. But things then change. The chapters in Part 2 are all set mainly in 1958, but each has an introductory section set in 1985. The Part 3 chapters are different again. They are all set completely in 1985, while depicting the Losers as they visit places recalled from their 1950s childhoods.

Part 4 is much like Part 2 (1958 chapters with a 1985 lead-in). In Part 5, the chapter sections go back and forth between 1985 and 1958 more or less unpredictably as the action in the two years becomes very similar. In fact, there are Part 5 sections in which the reader is deliberately left in doubt as to the year.

I believe this structural description of the five parts of *IT* reveals a gradual merging of the action in 1958 and 1985. The two years are initially described in separate chapters, but then 1985 begins to penetrate chapters that are mainly set in 1958. Also, the presence of 1958 is strongly felt in chapters set mainly in 1985. Finally, we're not even sure whether we're in 1958 or 1985. To my mind, this expresses the idea that the child Losers and adult Losers are gradually becoming more integrated with one another. It's a structural equivalent of the psychological, social and supernatural redemption that they strive for in both 1958 and 1985.

There's an important observation to make about the restructuring of novels for expressive effect – a warning in fact. Storytelling, especially in popular fiction, has evolved certain structures that are highly effective and extremely familiar to the reading public. Earlier, I mentioned the three-act structure with its clearly-defined beginning middle and end. This is really the rock-solid foundation for the vast majority of stories in popular fiction and movies. By varying those structures for the purpose of expressing theme, an author may be in danger of stretching the story into an unfamiliar and less effective shape. Looking specifically at *IT* and the author's use of structure to express the principle of repetition, the risk is clear: the novel could have simply ended up repeating itself in a tedious manner. The most obvious way that Stephen King has avoided this risk is to place the years a long way apart. In spite of the similar outline and near-identical climaxes of the action in the two years, it's obvious that describing childhood in the 1950s and adulthood in the 1980s will involve distinctly different characterisation, settings and situations. But I'd also like to discuss a couple of special effects that Stephen King uses to inject energy and interest into the 1958/1985 repetition structure.

The first of these techniques occurs regularly in Part 2 and Part 4 of the novel. At the end of each 1985 section at the start of a chapter, the last sentence cuts off and then continues in the 1958 section that follows. Here's the Chapter 4, section 1, transition to section 2, for example.

> ... Ben Hanscom's pupils contract at the command of his dreaming brain, which sees not the darkness which lies over western Illinois but the bright sunlight of a June day in Derry, Maine, twenty-seven years ago.
> Bells.
> The bell.
> School.
> School is.
> School is
> [Section 2]
> out!
> The sound of the bell went burring up and down the halls of Derry School ...

The beginning of the sentence is Ben in 1985 thinking back to his school days. The end of the sentence is Ben in 1958 actually living his school days. It's like a cinematic scene change with a bridging voiceover or an element such as a sound effect shared by the two scenes. Rather cleverly, it increases the sense that the past is beginning to break into the world of the grown-up Losers.

Let's move on to a second, equally innovative technique used to enliven the novel's pattern of alternation between 1958 and 1985. You'll no doubt have noticed the italics used in the 1985 sections at the start of each chapter in parts 2 and 4. Italics are usually a style reserved for internal monologue, so its use here for narration of normal activity brings a feeling of distance or unreality to the events of 1985. In my view, it expresses the idea that repetition of old mistakes over and over again leads to a feeling of inauthenticity. The events of 1958 are rendered in non-italic type, and therefore feel authentic and true by comparison with the 1985 events. The implication is clear. Finding a way out of repetitive problem behaviour is the path to a more authentic life. It will require that the characters revisit their past and recover important truths about themselves or their personal traumas.

A third technique is limited to a single key moment at the point where the 1958 and 1985 narratives converge. In Chapter 22, section 2, set in 1958, we witness a strange, psychic duel between Bill and 'It'. Just two sections later, in section 4, we're in 1985 with almost identical events taking place. The risk of tedious repetition is obvious, but Stephen King manages to keep us fully engaged with the 1985 account, and he does so by making relatively small changes to the narrative style. Most obviously, he adopts a new viewpoint. Although both the and 1958 and 1985 accounts take us to the same vague metaphysical space called 'the deadlights', the author augments this with a surprisingly different perspective in 1985. That is to say, the 1985 passage momentarily steps out of the deadlights and describes the Losers watching the inert bodies of Bill and 'It' (in the form of a spider). The duel is somehow taking place inside the heads of those two characters.

> The other four watched, paralyzed. It was an exact replay of what had happened before – at first. The Spider, which seemed about to seize Bill and gobble him up, grew suddenly still. Bill's eyes locked with Its ruby ones. There was a sense of contact … a contact just beyond their ability to divine. But they felt the struggle, the clash of wills.

We soon step back into the psychic conflict, but without the feeling that we're going over exactly the same ground.

The lesson is clear, if you decide to experiment with structure in big and dramatic ways – for example by alternating between timeframes from chapter to chapter – you will almost certainly need to call on a toolbox of micro-techniques to ensure that the reader remains engaged and entertained.

Narrative Thread Patterns

It's not just the subdivisions of the novel that are used to express thematic material in *IT*. Stephen King also uses the relationships between plot strands expressively. He even plays with the story spine in order to convey thematic meaning.

You'll recall that I identified Georgie's death and Bill's subsequent guilt as the novel's spine. However, it seems to me that the author has provided us with at least one other credible candidate for that job: the plot strand relating to the Losers' promise that they will return to Derry if necessary. Several spine-like qualities make it stand out from the list of subplots. It clearly has a special status, given that it's extensively discussed by Mike in the first two interludes. It's also linked to some very important plot points. Firstly, it triggers Mike's call to each of the Losers (Chapter

3), and, secondly, it's the motivation behind the meeting at the Chinese restaurant (Chapter 10). The importance of this latter event is emphasised by the fact that it occurs at the all-important midpoint of the novel.

However, there are important reasons why the promise plot strand could never be the story spine. Firstly, it's not mentioned until Chapter 3). Although that's somewhat close to the start of the novel, the Bill and Georgie strand occupies the whole of the very first chapter. A vivid sequence of scenes describes the lead up to Georgie's death, the event itself and the aftermath. By contrast, we only get a direct and complete account of the promise towards the end of the novel – after the apparent resolution of the central struggle with 'It'. As the adult Losers are exiting the tunnels, we hear how the child Losers were afraid that they may not have defeated 'It' completely. As a result, they commit themselves to return if necessary (Chapter 23, section 9). This leads me to a second reason why the promise plot strand could never be a credible story spine. It would be difficult to argue that the promise plot initiates the novel's central conflict – the struggle with 'It' – given that it only occurred after the 1958 showdown in the tunnels. By contrast, Bill has implicitly been engaged in a struggle with 'It' since 1957.

It seems to me that the promise plot is actually a ghostly reflection of the true spine. It has some of the power to motivate key plot developments, but it doesn't provide an essential impetus to the story's central conflict or form part of the resolution to that conflict. It floats free in the story. I would argue that this dislocation of a would-be story spine is in fact an ingenious expression of the major theme within the novel, namely the futility of repeating problem behaviour over and over again. After all, what is the fulfilment of the 27-year-old promise but a wasteful rerun of a battle that should have been won in 1958?

I was careful, earlier, to warn against ill-considered experimentation with the building blocks that make up a familiar three-act narrative. Similarly, experimentation with story spine structure is not normally recommended. Even if you have the technical ability to bring it off, there needs to be a very compelling reason for considering it, given that the story spine is quite literally the pillar that holds up an entire novel. A misstep could bring the whole thing crashing down for the reader. Nevertheless, Stephen

King has shown what's possible with careful manipulation of our expectations about novel structure.

Set-up and Pay-off Patterns

To conclude this appendix, I want to look at a group of structures that I collectively refer to as 'set-up and pay-off'. These too are used extensively to dramatise the thematic material of *IT*.

The standard set-up and pay-off structure is extremely common in all literary and movie genres. It involves presenting the reader with an apparently innocuous piece of information at one point in the story, then, later in the story, showing the same information in a way that reveals its true importance. A memorable example is found in just about every James Bond movie ever made. They typically have a scene close to the start when the technical guy, Q, talks Bond through the capabilities of some new spy gadgets. One of these secret weapons will remain forgotten for most of the movie, but Bond will eventually find himself in dire peril and realise that it's just the thing he needs. During a set-up sequence – in other words, the episode when our attention is first drawn to a phenomenon that will later become significant – questions will probably occur to us. Why are we being told this? What role will it play? But it's usually only a mild form of suspense based on simple curiosity. When we encounter the same phenomenon for a second time, during the pay-off, we get a sudden thrill of comprehension as well as a satisfying sense of completion.

This standard type of set-up and pay-off is not a prominent feature of *IT*. In fact, it's strangely absent from the novel. Its ubiquity in popular storytelling of all kinds would lead you to expect a few examples, but they don't exactly leap off the page. However, Stephen King does provide us with two fascinating variations on the set-up and pay-off structure, and it's very clear that he has done so in order to express thematic meaning – specifically, the theme of repeating behaviour.

Stephen King's set-up and pay-off variations play with three characteristics of the standard version:

1. When the phenomenon first appears, it arises naturally out of the story events but there's no specific information to suggest its future importance – it seems routine or innocuous.
2. Time passes between the first appearance of the phenomenon

and the second appearance.

3. The pay-off involves the character seeing a value or significance to the phenomenon that was previously not apparent.

The first variation interferes with the first of those characteristics. In the 1957/1958 sections of the novel, we are occasionally shown a vague foreshadowing of something that will go on to become important in the future (in the novel's timeframe). A typical example would be the following cryptic references to the Turtle in Chapter 1, section 2, which takes place in 1957.

> George sifted through the junk on the shelf as fast as he could – old cans of Kiwi shoepolish and shoepolish rags, a broken kerosene lamp, two mostly empty bottles of Windex, an old flat can of Turtle wax. For some reason this can struck him, and he spent nearly thirty seconds looking at the turtle on the lid with a kind of hypnotic wonder.

The meaning of Georgie's fascination with the turtle image is absolutely opaque at the time. We will only later come to understand its significance – during the 1958 confrontation with 'It'. That is many months of novel time (and 1000 pages) after the turtle wax moment. So far so similar to the standard set-up and pay-off. But there the similarity ends. In this structure, the initial mention of the turtle image could in no way be classed as routine or innocuous. It doesn't arise naturally out of the story events at all. In fact, it has a haunting weirdness that leaves us with an uneasy sense of some hidden agenda at work in the universe. This is quite different from the mild suspense of a traditional set-up and pay-off. Even when the pay-off comes, the mystery isn't dispelled. We still wonder how Georgie could have foreseen the existence of the Turtle. It may even have crossed your mind (as it did mine) that he became aware of this strange creator figure in a time before the events of the novel, but that's never confirmed. It's a disorienting effect that mimics the experience of helplessly repeating problem behaviours – a queasy feeling of being controlled by forces that seem alien but plainly come from your own mind.

The second variation on the set-up and pay-off structure is much more commonly seen in *IT*. This technique plays with the second of the characteristics listed above – the passage of time between appearances of a piece of information. Essentially, it involves some event in the past being recollected only vaguely to begin with (the set-up), but then, further on in the novel, being recollected and reported in vivid detail (the pay-off). Unlike the traditional structure, the pay-off sequence in this variation occurs in the past relative to the set-up. In *IT*, it's easy to see why this structure appears so frequently in the novel. The adult Losers' are determined to revisit the largely forgotten events of their childhood, but they're struggling with a strange amnesia. As a result, the early parts of the novel are filled with vague perceptions of things in the past. In Chapter 3, section 2, for example, Richie struggles to recall details of the Losers' promise to return to Derry if necessary.

> 'I made a promise. We all promised that we would go back if the something started happening again. And I guess it has.'
> 'What something are we talking about, Rich?'
> 'I'd just as soon not say.' Also, you'll think I'm crazy if I tell you the truth: I don't remember.
> 'When did you make this famous promise?'
> 'A long time ago. In the summer of 1958.'

Contrast this muddle-headed account with the vivid, direct description of the promise during the subsequent pay-off. It comes in Chapter 23, section 9, right after the apparent destruction of 'It' in 1958.

> 'Swuh-Swear to muh-me that you'll c-c-c-come buh-back,' Bill says. 'Swear to me that if Ih-Ih-It isn't d-d-dead, you'll cuh-home back.'
> 'Swear,' Ben said.
> 'Swear.' Richie.
> 'Yes – I swear.' Bev.
> 'Swear it,' Mike Hanlon mutters.
> 'Yeah. Swear.' Eddie, his voice a thin and reedy whisper.
> 'I swear too,' Stan whispers, but his voice falters and he looks down as he speaks.
> 'I-I swuh-swuh-swear.'

Highly specific words and gestures paint a detailed emotional and physical picture of the event in 1958. The past has come fully into focus.

Sometimes, that strange amnesia can't explain the descriptive vagueness of a passage introducing some phenomenon from 1958. For example, you would think that Mike – the man who personally called the other Losers requesting that they fulfil their childhood promise – would be willing and able to give a fairly detailed description of the promise from the word go. But this is apparently not the case. Mike's earliest reference to the promise event fails to provide a full picture of the dramatic setting. It's positively nebulous, in fact.

> I think of us standing in the water, hands clasped, making that promise to come back if it ever started again – standing there almost like Druids in a ring, our hands bleeding their own promise, palm to palm.

Where did this occur? What was the context that made it seem necessary? How did people behave as they spoke the promise? What precise words were spoken? We do not receive answers to these questions for many chapters. It seems to me that the author has artificially withheld this information about the promise when the character had every reason to share it. I believe he does so in order to ensure a vivid and memorable pay-off scene when the promise is directly described.

Now we come to the third variation. It plays with the third set-up and pay-off characteristic listed above and, in a sense, it's the opposite of the technique just described. In this variation, we initially receive a detailed account of a phenomenon in the past. Then, further on in the novel, that phenomenon is briefly vaguely alluded to in hindsight. One example begins in Chapter 6, section 5. We receive a long, idyllic account of the agricultural year on the Hanlon farm around 1958. The passage is bursting with detail and forms the backdrop to a major plot point, namely Mike's encounter with a monstrous bird. This vivid and terrifying episode is still kicking around in our minds two chapters later, in Chapter 8, section 1, when we hear about the Hanlon place again. This time, the farm is mentioned only briefly and incidentally.

> … somewhere along there between the Rhulin Farms and town he would drive past the Bowers place and then the Hanlon place.

Richie just happens to be driving into Derry in 1985 when he sees Mike Hanlon's family home. It may be an incidental mention

178

contained in a single phrase, but its effect is to evoke the 1958 description from two chapters previously. As a result, it seems heavy with significance. This effect, once again, dramatises the novel's theme of repetition. It's like the faint echo of an old trauma ringing through the years.

The most condensed expression of this technique is seen in Chapter 6, section 4. Mike is out on his bike in 1958.

> He turned right on Jackson Street, bypassing downtown, and then crossed to Main Street by way of Palmer Lane – and during his short ride down this little byway's one-block length he passed the house where he would live as an adult. He did not look at it; it was just a small two-story dwelling with a garage and a small lawn. It gave off no special vibration to the passing boy who would spend most of his adult life as its owner and only dweller.

Once again, the 1958 narrative is brimming over with detail and personal meaning – this is the last moment of innocence before the terrifying encounter with the bird. But then we are suddenly jerked into the future as the narration notes that Mike is riding past the house where he would be living in 1985. There is no gap at all between the set-up and pay-off episodes in this case. It's almost as though Mike's life, dominated by a lonely, repetitive vigil, has collapsed in on itself so that past, present and future are all one thing.

In Chapter 23, section 8, the author manages to combine two set-up and pay-off structures in a moment of powerful collision between past and present. As the grown-up Losers leave the tunnels, Bill bumps into a kid.

> A kid in a red rainslicker and green rubber boots was sailing a paper boat along the brisk run of water in the gutter. He looked up, saw them looking at him, and waved tentatively. Bill thought it was the boy with the skateboard – the one whose friend had seen Jaws in the Canal.

Clearly, on one level, we're seeing a revenant of Georgie as he was at the beginning of the novel. In that sense, Bill is experiencing one of those incidental moments that recalls a significant time and place in the past, as per variation 3.

On another level, the 1985 appearance of a Georgie revenant

could be seen as one of those pay-off moments when the true meaning of some cryptic phenomenon from the past is unveiled (as per variation 1). I say that because two mind-boggling possibilities occur to me when I read the passage about the boy with the slicker and the paper boat in Chapter 23, section 8. Firstly, I begin to wonder whether 'It' is dead after all. Perhaps this new kid is about to be dragged into a gutter or suffer some equally nasty fate. If that is the case, we are finally seeing the death of Georgie in its true light – as just one point in a repeating sequence of identical deaths that extends into the future. The second possibility is the idea that the 1957 storm during which Georgie died was actually the apocalyptic aftermath of a previous attack on 'It' – the closing sequence of an adventure experienced by other kids in a hypothetical story before the scope of this novel.. Once again, Georgie's death is effectively gaining a whole new significance thanks to the inclusion of a second boy in a second rain storm 28 years later. So, in at least two ways, the events of Chapter 23, section 8, correspond closely to set-up and pay-off variation 1 described above.

Like so many of Stephen King's variations on the set-up and pay-off structure, this passage hovers on the edge of one's ability to fully explain the nuances of thematic meaning. But that elusiveness is part of its significance, since it mimics the disorientation and amnesia of a life or society that repeats its mistakes over and over again.

Takeaway

- The novel's thematic material is expressed through patterns created with the text's subdivisions and narrative threads. These patterns are specific to the themes in *IT* but may act as an inspiration for your own structural expressions of theme.
    - Subdivision patterns
        - Micro-scenes that contain some encounter with 'It' break into the text, expressing the theme of subterranean evil.
        - Allowing two years to run in parallel draws our attention to the repetitiousness of events.
        - The merging of the action of 1958 and 1985 expresses the idea of escape from repetition.
        - Various special effects ensure that the story is

not pulled into an unentertaining shape by the desire to express thematic meaning.

o Narrative thread patterns

- The presence of an orphaned story spine alongside the real one expresses the futility of the characters' repetitious behaviours.

o Set-up and pay-off patterns

- The standard set-up and pay-off structure presents a phenomenon in such a way that it looks innocuous, but it later reveals the phenomenon's special significance.

- Variations on the traditional set-up and pay-off variations play with three characteristics of the standard version.

  - The set-up becomes weird and prescient rather than innocuous.

  - The pay-off is located in the past relative to the set-up.

  - At the pay-off, there is a brief but poignant reference to the more elaborate details provided in the set-up.

APPENDIX 2: ACT-STRUCTURE COMPARISON

Five-Act Structure (Freytag)	Three-Act Structure (*Save the Cat*)
Exposition: The characters, settings and main challenge are introduced.	Act 1 'set-up': The protagonist's normal life. Act 1 'catalyst': An event that challenges the protagonist. Act 1 'debate': The protagonist works through their doubts.
Rising action: The characters struggle with obstacles as they deal with the main challenge.	Act 2 'break into 2': The protagonist commits to the challenge. Act 2 'fun and games': The meat of the story.
Climax: A high point of tension that represents a major turning point.	Act 2 'midpoint': A false victory or defeat.
Falling action: Consequences felt, twists revealed, unknown details become known.	Act 2 'bad guys close in': Increasing trouble for the protagonist. Act 2 'all is lost': Another false

	victory or defeat (the inverse of the midpoint). Act 2 'dark night of the soul': The protagonist searches for a solution to their troubles.
Denouement: The resolution of the main challenge.	Act 3 'break into 3': The protagonist understands what they need to do. Act 3 'finale': The protagonist puts their plan into action.

SPECIAL OFFER

A comprehensive set of exercises accompanies *Write Like Stephen King*. The 20-page workbook will walk you through the process of planning a novel in the style of Stephen King, and help you practise techniques specific to the horror genre.

To receive the writing exercises for FREE, all you have to do is sign up for my *Popular Fiction Masterclass* email newsletter. Go to the Web address below, then follow the on-screen instructions.

http://popularfictionmasterclass.com/1059-73/

THANK YOU FOR CHOOSING THIS BOOK

If you enjoyed reading it and working through the exercises, I'd be delighted if you could leave a review on Amazon. Positive feedback from readers helps me a great deal and it's always great to hear what like-minded people think of my work. Go to the Web address below, then click on the image of this book. You'll be taken to the relevant Amazon page.

http://popularfictionmasterclass.com/about/

It would also be great to see you on my Facebook page. That's where we continue the discussion of subjects raised in the *Popular Fiction Masterclass* series of books.

https://www.facebook.com/pfmasterclass/

To browse other titles in this series, please go to the following Web address.

http://popularfictionmasterclass.com/about/

43463238R00116

Made in the USA
Middletown, DE
24 April 2019